The Complete Vegetarian Cookbook

APPLE

First published in the UK in 2006 by
Apple Press
Sheridan House
114 Western Road
Hove
East Sussex BN3 1DD
United Kingdom
www.apple-press.com

©Richard Carroll

Complete Vegetarian Cookbook

Publisher: Richard Carroll
Production Manager: Anthony Carroll
Cover Designer: Aisling Gallagher
Text Designer: Lucy Adams
Food Photography: Steve Baxter, Phillip Wilkins, David Munns, Thomas
Odulate, Christine Hanscomb and Frank Wieder
Home Economists: Sara Buenfeld, Emma Patmore, Nancy McDougall, Louise
Pickford, Jane Stevenson, Oded Schwartz, Alison Austin and Jane Lawrie
Food Stylists: Helen Payne, Sue Russell, Sam Scott, Antonia Gaunt
and Oded Schwartz
Recipe Development: Terry Farris, Jacqueline Bellefontaine, Becky Johnson,
Valerie Barrett, Emma Patmore, Geri Richards,
Pam Mallender and Jan Fullwood
Nutritional Consultant: Moya de Wet BSc SRD
Proof Reader: Kate Evans

Includes Index

ISBN-10: 1 84543 169 3
ISBN-13: 978 1 84543 169 3

Printed in Singapore

CONTENTS

Introduction

Vegetarian eating is a healthy alternative for today's lifestyle. Meals without meat, poultry or seafood are attractive, tasty and satisfying – as well as being good for you. The recipes in this book are for delectable dishes which can be combined, or can be enjoyed as a hearty meal on their own.

Perfect veggies

Influenced by cuisines from around the world, the recipes in this book are for easy-to-prepare dishes which have the wonderful texture and flavour of fresh vegetables, raw and cooked.

From an Asian-influenced soup to scrumptious desserts, this selection of satisfying and delicious recipes will enable you to prepare natural healthy food to suit every appetite and for every occasion, from a quick snack to a three-course dinner party.

Vegetable know-how

To make the most of your garden-fresh vegetables, we have put together essential step-by-step preparation and cooking tips to help you create delicious veggie dishes.

| Cubed | Diced | Minced | Grated | Sliced |

Ready

Easy cooking and preparation depends on having a few good basic pieces of equipment. To make life easier for you, it is worth investing a little time and money in some good equipment such as a large chopping board; a small sharp vegetable or paring knife, as well as several larger sharp knives for cutting and chopping; a grater; a vegetable peeler and a colander or large sieve. Remember to keep your knives sharp: either learn to sharpen them yourself or take them to a knife sharpener regularly. Sharp knives make preparation a breeze.

Set

Wash vegetables before preparing, but do not soak. Soaking tends to draw out the valuable water-soluble vitamins and you end up with vegetables with a lower nutrient content. As with most rules there are always exceptions and it may be necessary to soak very dirty vegetables to remove dirt and creepy-crawlies.

If this is the case, always keep soaking times to a minimum.

- Vegetables that are left whole with their skins on have a higher nutrient and fibre content than those that are finely chopped and peeled. Many of the precious vitamins and minerals found in vegetables are stored just under the skin. Only peel vegetables if necessary.

- For maximum nutritional value, prepare vegetables just before cooking and serve as soon as they are cooked.

- The smaller the portion, the quicker the cooking time. For example, grated carrot will cook more quickly than carrot cut into slices.

Go

Here's how:

- To cube, cut into about 1cm pieces.
- To dice, cut into 0.5cm pieces.
- To mince, cut into 0.25cm pieces.
- To grate, use either a hand grater or a food processor with a grating attachment.
- To slice, cut very thin or thick.
  You can also slice into rings. Another way to slice is to cut diagonally. This is a good way to prepare vegetables such as carrots, celery and zucchini for stir-frying.

Remember the three Ms

- Minimum water
- Minimum cooking
- Minimum cutting

VEGETABLE	SERVE	FIBRE
Asparagus, boiled	6-8 spears(60g)	1.4
Beans, green, raw	$^{1}/_{2}$ cup (6g)	1.2
Bean sprouts	2 tbsps (10g)	0.3
Beetroot, canned	2 slices (20g)	0.6
Broccoli, boiled	$^{2}/_{3}$ cup (100g)	3.9
Cabbage, white, boiled	$^{1}/_{2}$ cup (50g)	1.0
Capsicum, green, raw	$^{1}/_{4}$ capsicum (40g)	0.5
Carrot, peeled, boiled	1 carrot (100g)	2.9
Cauliflower, boiled	$^{2}/_{3}$ cup (100g)	2.0
Celery, raw	1 stalk (100g)	0.8
Chilli, raw	2 chillies (5g)	0.6
Cucumber, peeled, raw	4-5 slices (20g)	0.1
Eggplant, baked	$^{1}/_{2}$ small (75g)	2.7
Garlic, raw	2 cloves (10g)	1.7
Leek, boiled	1 leek (50g)	1.4
Lettuce, raw	2 leaves (20g)	0.1
Mushrooms, fried	4-6 mushrooms (75g)	1.4
Olives	3 green (20g)	0.8
Onion, peeled, fried	1 onion (80g)	2.2
Parsley	2 sprigs (2g)	0.1
Peas, green, boiled	$^{1}/_{3}$ cup (40g)	1.0
Potato, peeled, roasted	1 medium (120g)	2.4
Potato, unpeeled, boiled	1 medium (120g)	3.0
Pumpkin, peeled, boiled	$^{1}/_{2}$ cup (80g)	2.4
Radish, red, raw	2 radishes (10g)	0.1
Silverbeet, boiled	3 stalks (100g)	2.1
Sweetcorn	$^{1}/_{2}$ cup kernels (70g)	3.5
Tomato, raw	1 medium (130g)	2.4
Zucchini, boiled	1 medium (110g)	1.5

* grams of dietary fibre per serve

Good for you

Health authorities recommend that we eat four serves of vegetables daily, at least one of which should be raw. The old adage of a white, a yellow and a green may be rarely taught these days, but it is a good reminder that the brightly coloured vegetables are usually the best source of vitamins. Most of the vitamin content lies just under the skin, so vegetables should be cooked and eaten with the skin on as often as possible.

Pantry planning

Try the following tips for no-fuss pantry planning.

- If you store herbs and spices in alphabetical order, they are easily located and you can quickly see when they need replacing.

- Growing a few herbs of your own such as basil, coriander, rosemary, mint, chives and parsley means that you always have these on hand. These fresh herbs are often the secret to delicate flavours in meals.

- Place all staples, such as sugar and flour, together. Store sauces and condiments according to favourite cuisines; just a glance in the cupboard will give you great ideas.

- Keep a good selection of frozen vegetables. Peas, beans, spinach and corn are great standbys and only take minutes to cook in the microwave.

- Keep a variety of breads and rolls in the freezer and defrost in the microwave for delicious instant sandwiches.

- Cooked pasta and rice freeze well; reheat in minutes in the microwave and save time on busy nights.

- Evaporated milk, available as full-cream or skim milk, is a terrific standby when there is no fresh cream. It can be used for sauces and quiches and it whips well when chilled. Store a few cans in the pantry for emergencies.

appetisers

GRILLED VEGETABLE BRUSCHETTA

Ingredients
1 red or yellow pepper, deseeded and
  sliced into strips
1 courgette, halved and thinly sliced lengthwise
1 red onion, thinly sliced
2 large plum tomatoes, thickly sliced
3 tbsp extra virgin olive oil

2 tsp wholegrain mustard
black pepper
1 ciabatta loaf cut into 8 slices, or 8 slices
  from a baguette
1 clove garlic, halved
8 pitted black olives, thinly sliced
fresh basil to garnish

Method
1 Preheat the grill to high and line the grill rack with foil. Place the pepper, courgette, onion and tomatoes in a bowl. Whisk together 2 tablespoons of oil, the mustard and black pepper, then pour over the vegetables and toss gently to coat.

2 Spread the vegetables in a single layer on the grill rack and grill for 3–4 minutes on each side, until lightly browned. Set aside and keep warm.

3 Toast the bread slices on both sides under the grill and while still hot, rub the garlic halves over one side of each piece of toast. Divide the vegetables between the toast slices, piling them onto the garlicky side. Scatter over the olives and drizzle over the remaining oil. Garnish with fresh basil and serve.

Serves 4

ROMAN KEBABS

Ingredients
1 French bread baton
400g mozzarella
4 tomatoes
75mL olive oil

1 tbsp lemon juice
1 tsp dried oregano
salt and black pepper
fresh basil to garnish

Method
1 Preheat the oven to 230°C/Gas Mark 8. Soak 4 wooden skewers in water for 10 minutes.

2 Cut the bread into 16 x 1cm thick slices and then cut the mozzarella into 12 slices. Slice each tomato into 3, discarding the ends.

3 Combine the oil, lemon juice, oregano and seasoning in a shallow dish. Generously brush both sides of the bread with the oil mixture, then thread the bread onto the skewers, alternating with the mozzarella and tomato slices and finishing with bread. Pour over any of the remaining oil mixture.

4 Place the kebabs on a baking sheet and cook for 6–8 minutes, carefully turning over halfway through, until the bread is crisp and the cheese just starting to melt. Cool slightly before serving garnished with the fresh basil.

Serves 4

GRILLED VEGETABLE BRUSCHETTA

RED ONION AND CHILLI TARTS

Ingredients
375g ready-rolled puff pastry
1 tbsp olive oil
200g red onions, halved
  and finely sliced lengthwise
1 small red chilli, deseeded and thinly sliced
salt and black pepper
2 tbsp red pesto
25g pine nut kernels

Method

1 Preheat the oven to 220°C/Gas Mark 7. Open out the pastry sheet and cut out 4 x 12cm rounds. Use a slightly smaller cutter or a sharp knife to score a 1cm border on each – this will form the rim. Place the rounds on a baking sheet.

2 Heat the oil in a large frying pan. Fry the onions for 10 minutes or until softened, stirring. Add the chilli and cook gently for 1 minute, then season.

3 Spread the pesto over the pastry rounds, leaving the rim clear. Spoon the onion mixture over the pesto and scatter with the pine nut kernels. Cook for 12–15 minutes, until the pastry has risen and is golden brown.

Serve 4

CREAMY CHICKPEA AND TOMATO DIP

Ingredients
250g dried chickpeas
6 tbsp olive oil, plus extra
  for drizzling (optional)
finely grated rind of $1/2$ lemon
  and juice of 2 lemons
350g plum tomatoes
2 cloves garlic, crushed
2 spring onions, finely chopped (optional)
3 tbsp finely chopped fresh parsley or mint
salt and black pepper

Method

1 Soak the chickpeas in cold water for 12 hours, or overnight. Drain and rinse thoroughly, then place in a saucepan and cover with fresh water. Bring to the boil and cook for 10 minutes, removing any foam with a slotted spoon. Reduce the heat and simmer, covered, for 1 hour or until tender.

2 Drain the chickpeas, reserving 6 tablespoons of the cooking water, and set a few chickpeas aside to garnish. in the food processor, blend the remaining chickpeas to a fairly smooth purée with the reserved cooking liquid, the oil and lemon juice. Transfer to a bowl.

3 Place the tomatoes in a bowl and cover with boiling water. Leave for 30 seconds, then peel, deseed and roughly chop. Add the tomatoes to the chickpea purée with the lemon rind, garlic, spring onions, and if using, the parsley or mint and seasoning.

4 Mix well and refrigerate for 30 minutes. Before serving, garnish with the reserved chickpeas and drizzle with olive oil, if desired.

Serve 4

BUBBLE AND SQUEAK WITH RED ONION CHUTNEY

Ingredients

675g potatoes, peeled and cut into
  even-sized pieces
1 garlic clove, peeled
125g Savoy cabbage, finely shredded
4 spring onions, finely sliced
sea salt and freshly ground
black pepper

25g butter
1 tbsp sunflower oil

For the onion chutney

2 large red onions, or 6 small red onions,
  finely chopped
50g golden sugar
1 tbsp white wine vinegar

Method

1 Place the potatoes and garlic in a saucepan and cover with water. Bring to the boil, cover and simmer for 15–20 minutes, until tender. Drain, return to the pan and mash until smooth. Cool.

2 Meanwhile, place the cabbage in a saucepan and pour over boiling water to just cover, bring back to the boil, then drain. Add the cabbage, spring onions and seasoning to the potato and mix well.

3 Place all the ingredients for the chutney in a saucepan and bring to the boil over a low heat. Simmer gently, uncovered, for about 20 minutes or until almost all of the liquid has evaporated.

4 Divide the potato into eight and shape into flat rounds. Melt the butter and oil in a frying pan and fry the cakes for 5 minutes on one side over a medium heat. Turn over, taking care as the cakes are quite soft, and cook for a further 5 minutes, until golden and heated through. Serve with the chutney.

Serves 4

ARTICHOKES WITH SOUR CREAM SAUCE

Ingredients

4 large globe artichokes
salt
284mL carton sour cream

5 spring onions, finely chopped
1 tbsp balsamic vinegar
1 clove garlic, finely chopped

Method

1 Cut off the artichoke stalks, so that the artichokes stand flat. Place in a large saucepan of boiling salted water and simmer, partly covered, for 40 minutes or until tender. To test if the artichokes are cooked, pull off an outside leaf – it should come away easily. Remove the artichokes from the pan and set aside for 30 minutes to cool.

2 Meanwhile, make the sauce. Mix together the sour cream, spring onions, vinegar and garlic. Pull the central cone of leaves out of each artichoke, leaving a wall of leaves around the edge; and discard central leaves. Scrape away the inedible core with a teaspoon, to leave the edible base.

3 Spoon plenty of sauce into the artichoke centre. Place the artichokes on plates and eat by plucking out a leaf and dipping it into the sauce. Use your teeth to pull away the edible fleshy part at the base of the leaf, then discard the rest.

Serves 4

GREEN VEGETABLE TERRINE WITH SALSA

Ingredients

100g peas
100g broad beans
125g thin asparagus spears,
 cut into 1cm pieces
2 savoy cabbage leaves, sliced
sunflower oil for greasing
4 large eggs
1 clove garlic, crushed
2 tsp ground coriander
350g ricotta cheese
6 tbsp coconut milk

3 tbsp double or whipping cream
1 tbsp chopped fresh coriander
1 tbsp chopped fresh basil,
 plus extra to garnish
salt and black pepper

For the salsa

3 tomatoes
1 ripe avocado, chopped
grated rind and juice of 1 lime
2 shallots, finely chopped
1 clove garlic, crushed
1 chilli, deseeded and chopped

Method

1 Bring a saucepan of lightly salted water to the boil. Cook the peas, broad beans, asparagus and cabbage for 3 minutes to soften, then refresh under cold running water, drain and set aside.

2 Preheat the oven to 180°C/Gas Mark 4. Grease a 450g loaf tin with the oil, line with baking paper and grease again. Whisk the eggs until foamy, then whisk in the garlic, ground coriander, ricotta, coconut milk and cream. Stir in the vegetables, then add the fresh coriander and basil. Season, then pour the mixture into the tin.

3 Place the loaf tin on a double layer of newspaper in a roasting tin. Pour boiling water into the roasting tin to reach halfway up the loaf tin. Cook for 50–55 minutes, until firm. Cool for 1 1/2 hours, then remove from the roasting tin, cover with foil and refrigerate for 2 hours or overnight.

4 Meanwhile, make the salsa. Put the tomatoes in a bowl, cover with boiling water and leave for 30 seconds. Remove, peel and deseed, then chop. Mix the tomatoes with the avocado, lime rind and juice, shallots, garlic and chilli, then season. Turn out the terrine, garnish with basil and serve with the salsa.

Serves 6

RICOTTA HERB DIP WITH GARLIC TOASTS

Ingredients

6 pitted green olives, finely chopped
1 tbsp chopped fresh tarragon
1 tbsp chopped fresh chives
1 tbsp chopped fresh mint
2 tsp finely grated lemon rind

250g tub ricotta cheese
black pepper
4 tbsp sun-dried tomato purée
1 large 5-cereal baguette, cut into
1cm thick slices
1 clove garlic, halved

Method

1 Mix together the olives, tarragon, chives, mint and lemon rind, then stir in the ricotta. Season with pepper and mix well. Lightly stir the sun-dried tomato purée into the ricotta mixture to create a marbled effect, then spoon into a serving dish.

2 Preheat the grill to high. Grill the baguette slices for 1–2 minutes on each side, until golden. Rub the cut surfaces of the garlic halves over the toast slices and serve them with the dip.

Serves 4

GRILLED BRIE WITH BEETROOT SALAD

Ingredients

1 avocado
250g pack cooked beetroot, drained and chopped
2 celery sticks, sliced
1 red dessert apple, cored and chopped
4 slices stonebaked white loaf
1 portion Dutch Brie, approx. 125g, quartered
120g pack Alfresco salad

For the dressing

3 tbsp extra virgin olive oil
3 tbsp cider vinegar
1 garlic clove, crushed
1 small red onion, finely chopped
1 tbsp tomato purée
sea salt and freshly ground
black pepper
25g pine nut kernels

Method

1 Peel and slice the avocado and place in a bowl together with the beetroot, celery and apple. Cover and set aside. Preheat the grill to high and lightly toast the bread for 2–3 minutes each side. Place a slice of Brie on top of each toast, then return them to the grill. Cook until the cheese is melted and slightly golden.

2 Meanwhile, to make the dressing, place all the ingredients in a small saucepan and bring to the boil, simmer for 2–3 minutes, until warmed through.

3 To serve, divide the salad leaves between four plates, top with the beetroot mixture and place a cheese toast on each plate. Drizzle over the warm dressing and serve immediately. Serves 4

BROCCOLI SOUFFLÉS WITH OLIVE PURÉE

Ingredients

butter for greasing
450g broccoli, chopped
284mL single cream
4 medium eggs, separated
salt and black pepper

For the Olive Purée

20 pitted black olives
100mL olive oil
grated rind and juice of 1 lemon

Method

1 Preheat the oven to 220°C/Gas Mark 7. Grease 4 individual ramekin dishes. Cook the broccoli in a little boiling salted water for 15 minutes until tender, then drain well. In a food processor, blend the broccoli to a smooth purée with the cream, egg yolks and seasoning. Transfer to a large mixing bowl.

2 Beat the egg whites until they increase in volume six-fold and form soft peaks. Gently fold one-third of the beaten whites into the broccoli purée, using a large metal spoon. Then, carefully fold in the remaining whites in two batches, mixing well.

3 Divide the mixture between the ramekin dishes and cook for 20–25 minutes, until risen and golden. Meanwhile, purée the olives, olive oil and lemon rind and juice in a food processor or with a hand blender. Serve with the soufflés.

Serves 4

WATERCRESS ROULADE WITH PARMESAN

Ingredients
vegetable oil for greasing
1 tbsp freshly grated Parmesan
85g watercress, finely chopped, thick
  stems discarded
4 medium eggs, beaten
salt and black pepper

For the filling
200g full-fat soft cheese, at room temperature
3 tbsp full-fat milk
85g bag watercress, finely chopped and thick stems
  discarded, with a few sprigs reserved to garnish
5 spring onions, finely chopped
salt and pepper

Method

1 Preheat the oven to 200°C/Gas Mark 6. Grease a 23 x 30cm swiss roll tin, line with baking paper, then sprinkle with half a tablespoon of Parmesan.

2 Mix together the watercress and eggs, season, then pour into the tin. Cook for 7–8 minutes, until the eggs have set. Remove from the oven and leave to cool for 5 minutes. Sprinkle over the remaining Parmesan. Lay a sheet of baking paper over the top and set aside for 35 minutes or until completely cool.

3 To make the filling, mix the soft cheese with the milk, watercress, onions and seasoning. Turn the cooled roulade onto a chopping board. Peel off the top sheet of paper, then spread the filling over the base. Roll up from the short end, peeling off the paper as you go. Refrigerate for 30 minutes, then serve in slices, garnished with watercress.

Serves 4

STUFFED TOMATOES

Ingredients
6 medium tomatoes
3/4 cup long-grain rice
1 tbsp butter
1 tbsp chopped onion

2 cups chicken stock
salt and freshly ground black pepper
3–4 canned anchovies, chopped
1 tbsp chopped basil
1 tbsp chopped parsley or chervil

Method

1 Cut the tops off the tomatoes, flip out seeds and hollow out a little with a small teaspoon. Chop tomato flesh. Stand tomato cups upside down to drain while you make the filling.

2 Wash and drain the rice. In a saucepan, heat the stock. Melt the butter in a saucepan and brown the onion. Add the rice and stir for about 3–4 minutes. Pour on the heated stock, add the chopped tomato flesh. Simmer covered until the stock is absorbed. Test if the rice is tender and, if not, cook a little longer. When the liquid is absorbed and rice just cooked, remove from the heat, fluff up rice. Stir in salt and pepper to taste and the chopped anchovies and herbs. Leave to cool and then fill the tomatoes with the rice mixture. Serve as a first course or as a light main dish with a green salad.

3 To serve hot, place tomatoes in an oiled ovenproof gratin dish, sprinkle with some Parmesan cheese and bake in a moderately hot oven (190°C) for 20 minutes or until heated through.

Serves 6

WATERCRESS ROULADE WITH PARMESAN

TOAST FINGERS WITH PESTO AND RICOTTA

Ingredients

**12 slices speciality bread, such as
  Grande Rustique, sliced**
3 tbsp olive oil

250g ricotta
5 tbsp pesto
black pepper
25g Parmesan cheese

Method

1 Toast the bread, then brush with a little oil. Meanwhile, beat together the ricotta and pesto, then stir in the rest of the oil. Season with pepper.

2 Cut the toast into fingers, discarding the ends. Spread with the ricotta mixture and shave over the Parmesan, using a vegetable peeler.

Serves 6

SWEET PEPPER TERRINE WITH BASIL VINAIGRETTE

Ingredients

butter for greasing
2 red and 2 yellow peppers, halved and deseeded
3 tbsp olive oil
I red chilli, deseeded and thinly sliced
250g ricotta
125g mature Cheddar cheese, grated
I tbsp Dijon mustard
I tsp salt

3 medium eggs, beaten
For the vinaigrette
2 tbsp white wine vinegar
2 tbsp extra virgin olive oil
4 tbsp sunflower oil
2 spring onions, finely sliced
3 tbsp finely chopped fresh basil
salt and black pepper

Method

1 Preheat the oven to 190°C/Gas Mark 5. Butter a large piece of baking paper and line a 450g loaf tin, leaving enough paper to cover the top. Finely dice half a red and half a yellow pepper and set aside. Roughly chop the rest of the pepper.

2 Heat the oil in a heavy-based saucepan, add the roughly chopped peppers and chilli, then cook, covered, for 20 minutes or until softened. Purée in a food processor or with a hand blender, then press through a sieve. Combine the ricotta, Cheddar, mustard, salt and eggs, then stir into the purée and diced peppers. Pour into the tin, then fold the paper over to cover the terrine without touching. Place the loaf tin in a roasting tin.

3 Pour in enough boiling water to reach halfway up the sides of the loaf tin, then cook for I hour and I5 minutes, adding more water if necessary. Cool for 2 hours, then place in the fridge for I hour. Invert onto a plate and peel off the paper. To make the vinaigrette, combine the ingredients, mixing well. Serve the terrine in slices with the vinaigrette.

Serves 4

SPICED OLIVES

Ingredients

1 pound green or ripe olives
1 fresh oregano sprig
1 fresh thyme sprig
1 teaspoon finely chopped fresh rosemary
2 bay leaves
1 teaspoon fennel seeds, bruised

1 tsp finely crushed
 cumin seeds
1 fresh red chilli, seeded
 and chopped
4 garlic cloves, crushed
olive oil

Method

1 Using a small sharp knife, make a lengthwise slit through to pit of each olive. Put olives into a bowl. Stir in oregano, thyme, rosemary, bay leaves, fennel seeds, cumin seeds, chilli and garlic.

2 Into a jar with a tight-fitting lid, pack olive mixture. Add enough oil to cover olives, seal and leave at least 3 days, shaking jar occasionally, before using.

Makes 6 servings

SUN-DRIED TOMATO AND CHEESE PUFFS

Ingredients

75g butter
175g plain flour, sifted
1/2 tsp salt
4 medium eggs, beaten
175g Gruyère, grated

For the stuffing
50g sun-dried tomatoes
 in oil, drained
50g butter

Method

1 Preheat the oven to 200°C/Gas Mark 6. Gently heat the butter and 225mL of water in a large saucepan for 5 minutes or until the butter has melted. Bring to the boil, then remove from the heat and stir in the flour and salt. Beat with a wooden spoon until the mixture forms a smooth ball.

2 Gradually add the eggs, beating well, until the dough is shiny. Stir in the Gruyère. Place balls of the dough (about 2 tablespoons to each ball) onto a baking sheet and cook for 20 minutes or until risen and browned. Turn off the oven. Cut a slit in the top of each puff to let the steam escape. Return the puffs to the cooling oven for 5 minutes, then remove and cool for a further 5 minutes.

3 Meanwhile, make the stuffing. Place the tomatoes and butter in a food processor and blend to a paste. Divide the paste between the puffs, packing it in with a teaspoon.

Makes 16

TZATZIKI (CUCUMBER WITH YOGHURT AND MINT)

Ingredients
185g plain Greek yoghurt
90g grated cucumber
1 tbsp lemon juice

1 clove garlic, crushed
salt and black pepper
1 tbsp chopped mint, optional

Method

1 Combine all the ingredients in a bowl. Cover the bowl with plastic wrap and refrigerate for at least 1 hour (to allow the flavours to develop).

2 Serve with pita bread as a dip, or as an accompaniment sauce.

Makes 1 cup

VEGETABLE TEMPURA

Ingredients
2 eggs
125mL ice-cold water
70g plain white flour, sieved
225g jar Cranberry and orange sauce, for dipping
vegetable oil, for deep-frying
1 courgette, cut into thick slices

1 large red onion, cut into wedges
225g broccoli, cut into small florets
1 red pepper, deseeded and cut into strips
125g green beans, topped only
125g asparagus, trimmed
sea salt
fresh basil leaves, to garnish (optional)

Method

1 To make the batter, lightly whisk together the eggs and water, then pour on to the flour all at once and whisk quickly, until the batter is smooth.

2 Heat the cranberry and orange sauce in a small saucepan, over a gentle heat, until warm and runny. Remove from the heat and place in a bowl.

3 Heat 5cm of oil in a wok or frying pan. Dip the vegetables in to the batter and coat well. Test the temperature of the oil by dropping in a little batter, if it floats straight back to the surface the oil is hot enough.

4 Deep-fry the vegetables in small batches for 3–4 minutes or until crisp and golden. Remove with a slotted spoon and drain on kitchen paper. Season with salt. If using, deep-fry a few basil leaves for 20 seconds, until crisp. Serve the vegetables immediately with the cranberry and orange sauce.

Serves 4

VINE TOMATOES AND GOATS' CHEESE BRUSCHETTA

Ingredients

450g small vine-ripened tomatoes
2 tbsp extra virgin olive oil
1 clove garlic, crushed
4 sprigs fresh thyme

4 thick slices ciabatta, cut
  on the diagonal
4 tbsp ready-made tapenade
100g soft goat's cheese, cut
  into chunks
fresh basil leaves to garnish

Method

1 Preheat the oven to 220°C/Gas Mark 7. Place the tomatoes, still on the vine, in a roasting tin and drizzle with the oil. Scatter over the garlic and thyme sprigs. Roast for 15 minutes or until the tomatoes are tender. Divide the tomatoes into 4 portions of roughly the same size, each still attached to part of the vine.

2 Meanwhile, preheat the grill to high. Toast the bread on both sides until golden. Spread each slice with 1 tablespoon of tapenade, add a few chunks of goats' cheese and top with the tomatoes on the vine. Drizzle over the juices from the roasting tin and sprinkle with the basil leaves.

Serves 4

MIXED MUSHROOMS ON HERBED MUFFINS

Ingredients

500g mixed mushrooms,
  including wild, oyster and shiitake
2 tbsp olive oil
salt and black pepper
25g butter
1 clove garlic, crushed
3 tbsp chopped fresh parsley

3 tbsp finely snipped chives,
  plus extra whole chives to garnish
2 tsp sherry vinegar or balsamic
  vinegar
4 tbsp low-fat soft cheese
3 English white muffins

Method

1 Halve any large mushrooms. Heat 2 teaspoons of the oil in a heavy-based frying pan, then add all the mushrooms, season lightly and fry over a medium to high heat for 5 minutes or until they start to release their juices.

2 Remove the mushrooms and drain on kitchen towels, then set aside. Add the rest of the oil and half the butter to the pan and heat until the butter melts. Add the garlic and stir for 1 minute.

3 Return the mushrooms to the pan, then increase the heat to high and fry for 5 minutes or until they are tender and starting to crisp. Stir in the remaining butter and 2 tablespoons each of parsley and chives, drizzle with the vinegar and season.

4 Mix the soft cheese with the remaining parsley and snipped chives. Split and toast the muffins. Spread the soft cheese mixture over the muffin halves and place on serving plates. Top with the mushrooms and garnish with the whole chives.

Serves 6

HUMMUS WITH VEGETABLE CRUDITÉS

Ingredients

400g canned chickpeas, drained
  and rinsed
juice of I lemon
3 tbsp extra virgin olive oil
2 tbsp light tahini
I clove garlic, crushed
$1/2$ tsp ground coriander

$1/2$ tsp ground cumin
black pepper
500g mixed vegetables; choose
  from peppers, carrots, courgettes,
  cauliflower, broccoli, mushrooms,
  radishes, baby asparagus and
  spring onions

Method

1 In a food processor (or with a handblender), blend the chickpeas, lemon juice, olive oil, tahini, garlic, coriander, cumin and black pepper until they form a coarse paste.

2 Slice the peppers, carrots and courgettes into sticks, and cut the cauliflower and broccoli into florets. Wipe the mushrooms and trim the radishes, asparagus and spring onions. Arrange the vegetables on a serving plate. Spoon the hummus into a serving bowl and serve with the crudités.

Serves 4

CARAMELISED SHALLOT AND ASPARAGUS TOASTS

Ingredients

3 tbsp olive oil
300g shallots, thickly sliced
2 cloves garlic, thickly sliced
I red chilli, deseeded and
  sliced (optional)
$1 1/2$ tbsp soft dark-brown sugar
2 tbsp dark soy sauce

I tbsp white wine vinegar
  or cider vinegar
150ml white wine
100g asparagus tips
4 plum tomatoes
juice of $1/2$ lemon
12 thick slices French bread
flat-leaf parsley or coriander
  to garnish

Method

1 Heat the oil in a wok or large, heavy-based frying pan. Add the shallots, garlic and chilli (if using) and stir-fry for 4–5 minutes, until they start to colour. Add the sugar and the soy sauce and stir-fry for 3–4 minutes, until the shallots are evenly browned.

2 Add the vinegar and wine to the shallots and bring to the boil. Reduce the heat and simmer, uncovered, for 8 minutes or until the shallots have softened and the liquid has thickened and looks glossy. Add the asparagus tips, cover, and cook for 4–5 minutes, until tender, stirring occasionally.

3 Place the tomatoes in a bowl and cover with boiling water. Leave for 30 seconds, then peel, deseed and chop. Add to the pan with the lemon juice, stir and heat for 1–2 minutes.

4 Meanwhile, preheat the grill to high. Toast the bread on both sides. Serve the toasts topped with the vegetable mixture and garnished with the parsley or coriander.

Serves 6

SPINACH AND GOAT'S CHEESE PITTA PIZZA

Ingredients

125g sun-dried tomatoes in oil,
   drained, plus 2 tbsp oil from the jar
2 tbsp tomato paste
1 clove garlic, roughly chopped
2 tsp finely chopped fresh thyme or

$^1/_2$ tsp dried thyme
250g baby spinach
6 mini pitta breads
6 cherry tomatoes, quartered
100g soft goat's cheese, sliced
1 tbsp sesame seeds

Method

1 Preheat the oven to 230°C. Blend the sun-dried tomatoes, tomato paste and garlic to a purée in a food processor or by using a hand blender. Mix in the thyme.

2 Bring a pan of water to the boil, immerse the spinach then remove and refresh in a bowl of cold water. Drain, then drizzle the sun-dried tomato oil over the top.

3 Spread the tomato and garlic purée over the pitta breads and top with the spinach. Scatter the cherry tomatoes over, along with the cheese and sesame seeds. Cook for 10 minutes or until the cheese has melted slightly and started to brown.

Serves 4

POTATO AND PARSLEY CROQUETTES

Ingredients

75g long-grain rice
2 large potatoes, cut into chunks
salt and black pepper
2 red onions, finely chopped

1 clove garlic, crushed
4 tbsp chopped fresh parsley
6 tbsp sesame seeds
sunflower oil for frying

Method

1 Cook the rice according to the packet instructions, until tender, then drain well. Spread on a plate and leave for 1 hour or until cooled completely, fluffing it up with a fork occasionally.

2 Meanwhile, put the potatoes into a large saucepan of boiling salted water, then simmer for 15–20 minutes, until tender. Drain, then mash. Put the mashed potato into a large bowl with the cooled rice, seasoning, onions, garlic and parsley. Mix thoroughly.

3 Shape the mixture into 8 croquettes with your hands, then roll in the sesame seeds. Heat 1cm of oil in a large, heavy-based frying pan and fry the croquettes for 2–3 minutes, turning until crisp and browned all over.

Serves 4

COURGETTE ROUNDS WITH RED PEPPER PURÉE

Ingredients

3 courgettes, grated

salt

4 tbsp snipped fresh chives,
  plus extra to garnish

2 tbsp chopped fresh coriander,
  plus extra leaves to garnish

$^1/_4$ tsp grated nutmeg

1 spring onion, finely chopped, to garnish

For the purée

3 tbsp olive oil

3 red peppers, cored, deseeded and chopped

salt and black pepper

Method

1 Sprinkle the courgettes with salt, place in a colander, then set aside for 30 minutes to draw out the excess moisture. Rinse under cold running water, then squeeze dry and mix with the chives, coriander and nutmeg. Pack the mixture into 4 ramekins – it should half-fill them. Refrigerate for 1 hour, or overnight.

2 To make the purée, put the oil into a saucepan, then add the peppers and season. Cook, covered, over a low heat for 15 minutes. Leave to cool for a few minutes, then blend to a smooth purée in a food processor, or with a hand blender. Press the purée through a sieve to remove the skins.

3 To serve, turn each ramekin onto a plate, giving it a sharp shake to dislodge the courgette round, then spoon around the sauce. Garnish with chives, coriander and spring onion.

Serves 4

GIANT CATHERINE WHEELS

Ingredients

400g shortcrust pastry

plain flour for dusting

100g mature Cheddar, grated

2 tbsp freshly grated Parmesan

2 tbsp tomato purée

2 tbsp pesto

1 medium egg, beaten,
  for glazing

vegetable oil for greasing

Method

1 Preheat the oven to 190°C/Gas Mark 5. Roll out the pastry on a floured surface and cut to make 2 rectangles measuring 20 x 25cm. Mix together the Cheddar and Parmesan, then set aside.

2 Spread 1 sheet of pastry with the tomato purée. Place the second sheet of pastry on top, spread with the pesto, then sprinkle with the cheese. Roll up the pastry from the shorter side with the filling inside. Brush the roll with the egg and refrigerate for 20 minutes.

3 Cut the roll into 1cm slices and place on greased baking sheets. Bake for 20 minutes or until golden. Leave to cool slightly on wire racks.

Makes 10

ROASTED RED PEPPER RAITA

Ingredients
2 red peppers
2 tsp cumin seeds
200g Greek yogurt

2 tbsp finely chopped fresh mint
salt and black pepper
1 tsp paprika to garnish

Method

1 Preheat the grill to high. Cut the peppers lengthwise into quarters, then remove the seeds and grill, skin-side up, for 10 minutes or until blackened and blistered. Place in a plastic bag and leave to cool for 10 minutes.

2 Meanwhile, preheat a wok and dry-fry the cumin seeds stirring constantly, over a high heat for 30 seconds, or until they start to pop. Remove the skins from the grilled peppers and discard, then roughly chop the flesh.

3 Mix the peppers with the yogurt, cumin seeds and mint and season to taste. Transfer to a serving dish and garnish with the paprika.

Serves 4

STUFFED TOMATOES WITH CHICKPEAS AND CORIANDER

Ingredients
2 slices day-old brown bread
4 large slicing tomatoes
1 clove garlic, crushed
100g canned chickpeas, drained
juice of 1 lemon
1 tbsp olive oil, plus extra
  for greasing

1 red onion, finely chopped
$3/4$ tsp cayenne pepper
1 tsp ground cumin
1 tsp ground coriander
4 tbsp chopped fresh coriander
salt and black pepper

Method

1 Preheat the oven to 160°C/Gas Mark 3. Place the bread in the oven for 20 minutes or until it becomes crisp. Process in a food processor to make breadcrumbs. Alternatively, use a grater. Increase the oven temperature to 200°C/Gas Mark 6.

2 Slice off the tomato tops and scoop out the insides. Place the shells upside-down on kitchen towels to drain. Put the insides and tops into a food processor with the garlic, chickpeas and lemon juice and blend to a purée.

3 Heat the oil, then cook the onion with the cayenne pepper, cumin and ground coriander for 4–5 minutes, until softened. Mix with the tomato mixture, breadcrumbs, fresh coriander and seasoning.

4 Spoon the mixture into the tomato shells. Place them on a lightly greased baking sheet and cook for 25 minutes or until the tomatoes are tender.

Serves 4

POTATO AND PARSNIP PUDDINGS WITH APPLE SAUCE

Ingredients
350g potatoes, peeled and coarsely grated
150g parsnips, peeled and coarsely grated
1 onion, finely grated
1 tbsp finely chopped
fresh sage or 1 tsp dried sage
1 medium egg, lightly beaten
4 tbsp dried breadcrumbs
salt and black pepper
2 tbsp olive oil

For the sauce
300g Bramley apples, peeled, cored and chopped
grated rind and juice of $1/2$ lemon
2 tbsp sugar or clear honey
1 tbsp finely chopped fresh sage or
  1 tsp dried sage
3–4 tbsp sour cream (optional)

Method

1 To make the puddings, place the potatoes, parsnips, onion, sage, egg, breadcrumbs and seasoning in a large bowl and mix together well. Cover and place in the fridge for 20 minutes.

2 Meanwhile, preheat the oven to 220°C/Gas Mark 7. To make the sauce, place the apples, lemon rind and juice and sugar or honey in a small, heavy-based saucepan with 2 tablespoons of water. Bring to the boil, cover, then reduce the heat and cook for 8–10 minutes or until the mixture forms a chunky purée. Remove from the heat and stir for 1 minute or until fluffy. Add the sage and sour cream, if using.

3 Brush 6 Yorkshire pudding tins with 1 tablespoon of the oil. Divide the pudding mixture between them, then brush the tops with half the remaining oil and cook for 15 minutes. Remove from the oven, brush with the remaining oil and cook for 5 minutes longer or until browned. Serve with the apple sauce.

Serves 6

THREE KINDS OF DEEP OF FRIED TOFU

Ingredients
1 block tofu, cut into 12 squares
arrowroot
3 tsps seaweed powder
3 tsps black sesame seeds
400mL udonji
chives

Method

1 Lightly roll tofu cubes in arrowroot.

2 Deep fry tofu for 3–4 minutes.

3 Roll 4 cubes in seaweed powder to coat and roll 4 cubes in black sesame seeds.

4 Place one seaweed, one black sesame seed and one plain tofu cube in each serving bowl.

5 Pour 100mL of udonji into each bowl. Garnish with chives and serve.

Serves 4

VEGETABLE BHAJIS

Ingredients
10 shallots, finely chopped
2 courgettes, coarsely grated
1 aubergine, finely diced
vegetable oil for frying
For the batter
100g chickpea flour
50g ground rice

¼ tsp bicarbonate of soda
1 tsp chilli powder
1 tsp turmeric
1–2 tbsp curry powder (mild or hot according to taste)
1 tsp salt

Method

1 To make the batter, put all the ingredients into a bowl, then gradually add 225mL of water, stirring constantly until combined. Add the shallots, courgettes and aubergine to the batter, mixing well.

2 Pour the oil into a wok to a depth of 5cm and heat over a medium to high heat. Check the oil is hot enough by dropping in a small piece of vegetable; it should sizzle. Gently place 4 balls of the mixture (about 2 tablespoons each) into the hot oil and fry for 2–3 minutes, until golden. Turn over and cook for a further 2–3 minutes, until crisp.

3 Remove the bhajis with a slotted spoon and drain on kitchen towels. Fry the remaining bhajis in the same way.

Serves 4

BAKED ONIONS WITH MUSHROOMS AND PINE NUTS

Ingredients
2 slices brown bread
4 large Spanish onions
2 tbsp olive oil
2 cloves garlic, choppeda

2 tbsp pine nut kernels
200g mushrooms, finely chopped
4 tbsp chopped fresh parsley
salt and black pepper

Method

1 Preheat the oven to 160°C/Gas Mark 3. Place the bread in the oven for 20 minutes or until it becomes crisp. Process in a food processor to make breadcrumbs. Alternatively, use a grater.

2 Meanwhile, slice the tops and bases off the onions. Place in a saucepan, cover with water and bring to the boil. Cook for 10 minutes to soften. Drain, then leave to cool for 20 minutes.

3 Increase the oven to 200°C/Gas Mark 6. Leaving the shell intact, cut out the middle of each onion, and finely chop. Heat the oil, then fry the garlic and chopped onion for 5 minutes. Add the pine nuts and mushrooms and fry for a further 5 minutes. Remove from the heat, then mix in the breadcrumbs, parsley and seasoning. Fill the onion shells with the mixture, then wrap each onion in foil, leaving the tops open. Place on a baking sheet and cook for 40 minutes or until the onions are tender.

Serves 4

ROASTED EGGPLANT AND GARLIC DIP

Ingredients
I large aubergine
5 cloves garlic, roasted
I tbsp tahini
I tbsp lemon juice
I tbsp olive oil
salt and black pepper

Method

1 Preheat the oven to 200°C.

2 Place the eggplant and garlic on a baking tray, drizzle with olive oil and roast in the oven for 20 minutes. Remove from the oven, scoop the flesh out of the inside of the eggplant, and place the flesh and roasted garlic in the bowl of a food processor.

3 Process until puréed, then add the tahini, lemon juice and olive oil, and process for a few seconds to combine.

4 Season to taste with salt and pepper, and serve with bread.

Makes 2 cups

TOMATO MOUSSE

Ingredients
I kg ripe red tomatoes
I tbsp tomato paste
salt and freshly ground pepper
2 tbsp gelatine
1/2 cup water
I cup cream
2 tbsp snipped chives
I tbsp finely chopped basil
sprigs of fresh basil or
watercress and cherry
tomatoes
to garnish

Method

1 Scald tomatoes, drain and drop in cold water then slip off skins. Cut into halves then scoop out the seeds into a coarse sieve. Place the drained juice and tomato halves in a food processor with the tomato paste, salt and pepper. Purée until smooth.

2 Sprinkle gelatine over water in a small pan and place over a gentle heat until dissolved. Stir all at once into the puréed tomato mixture and place in the fridge until well chilled. Stir every now and then while chilling and take out just on the point of setting. Whip the cream and fold it into the tomato mixture with the herbs. Spoon the mixture into 6 lightly oiled moulds (eg dariole moulds) and place immediately in the fridge to set. When firm unmould onto plates and serve garnished with basil or watercress and with the cherry tomatoes, tossed in a little dressing.

Serves 6

FENNEL AND ZUCCHINI CAKES

Ingredients

2/3 cup plain flour,
1 egg, separated
1 tbsp olive oil
75mL cold water
1/4 tsp salt and freshly

ground black pepper
250g fennel bulb
250g courgette
1 tbsp mint, chopped
oil, for shallow frying
garlic-flavoured natural yoghurt

Method

1 Sift the flour into a bowl and make a well. Into the well add the egg yolk, olive oil and cold water. Whisk the centre, gradually incorporating the flour (until a smooth batter has formed). Season with salt and pepper, cover, and leave to thicken for 30 minutes (in a cool place).

2 Grate the fennel and zucchini. Stir with the chopped mint into the batter. Whisk the egg-white until soft peaks form, and fold it gently into the batter mixture.

3 Shallow fry dessert spoonfuls of mixture (a few at a time). Cook until golden on both sides and cooked in the centre. Drain on paper towels.

4 Serve warm with garlic-flavoured natural yoghurt.

Serves 6

soups

PEA AND FRESH MINT SOUP

Ingredients

50g butter
2 rashers rindless streaky bacon, chopped
bunch of spring onions, chopped
450g shelled fresh peas, or frozen peas
2 Little Gem lettuces, shredded
salt and black pepper

2 tbsp chopped fresh mint
142mL carton single cream
pinch of caster sugar (optional)
fresh lemon juice (optional)
single cream to serve and snipped
  fresh chives to garnish

Method

1 Melt the butter in a large heavy-based saucepan. Add the bacon and cook for 2–3 minutes, then add the spring onions. Cover and cook gently for 5 minutes, stirring once or twice, until the onions have softened but not browned.

2 Add the peas and lettuce and 900mL of water. Season well, bring to the boil, then simmer for 10 minutes or until the vegetables are tender. Purée with the mint and cream until smooth, using a food processor or a hand blender.

3 Return the soup to the pan. Season again, if necessary, then add the caster sugar and lemon juice, if using. Reheat gently but do not allow the soup to boil. Serve in bowls with a spoonful of cream drizzled on top and a sprinkling of chives.

Serves 4

PLUM TOMATO, LENTIL AND BASIL SOUP

Ingredients

75g continental lentils
1 kg plum tomatoes
1 tbsp olive oil
2 onions, chopped
2 tbsp sun-dried tomato purée

750ml vegetable stock
1 bay leaf
black pepper
3 tbsp chopped fresh basil, plus extra
  leaves to garnish

Method

1 Rinse the lentils, drain, then add to a large saucepan of boiling water. Simmer, covered, for 25 minutes or until tender. Drain, rinse and set aside.

2 Meanwhile, place the tomatoes in a bowl, cover with boiling water, leave for 30 seconds, then drain. Remove the skins, deseed and chop. Heat the oil in a large saucepan, add the onions and cook for 10 minutes or until softened, stirring occasionally. Stir in the tomatoes, tomato purée, stock, bay leaf and black pepper. Bring to the boil and simmer, covered, stirring occasionally, for 25 minutes or until all the vegetables are cooked.

3 Remove the pan from the heat and cool for a few minutes. Remove and discard the bay leaf, then purée the soup until smooth in a food processor, liquidiser, or with a hand blender. Return to a clean pan, stir in the lentils and chopped basil, then reheat gently. Serve garnished with fresh basil.

Serves 4

WATERCRESS SOUP

Ingredients

I tbsp sunflower oil
4 shallots, finely chopped
I leek, thinly sliced
225g potatoes, diced
225g watercress, chopped

450mL vegetable stock
450mL half-fat milk
black pepper

Method

1 Heat the oil in a large saucepan, then add the shallots and leek and cook gently for 5 minutes or until softened, stirring occasionally. Add the potatoes and watercress to the shallot mixture and cook, stirring occasionally for a further 3 minutes or until the watercress wilts.

2 Stir in the stock, milk and black pepper. Bring to the boil, then reduce the heat and simmer, covered but stirring occasionally, for 20 minutes or until the potatoes are cooked and tender.

3 Remove the pan from the heat and cool for a few minutes. Purée the soup until smooth in a food processor, liquidiser, or with a hand blender. Return to a clean pan and reheat gently, until piping hot. Serve seasoned with coarsely ground black pepper.

Serves 4

AVOCADO GAZPACHO

Ingredients

2 large ripe avocados, stoned, peeled
  and chopped
grated rind and juice of 1 lemon
600mL vegetable stock
2 large tomatoes
1 cucumber, chopped

1 green and 1 red pepper, deseeded
  and chopped
1 clove garlic, crushed
salt and black pepper
4 tbsp freshly snipped chives to garnish

Method

1 Place the avocados, lemon rind and juice and the stock in a food processor and blend to a thin, smooth purée. Pour into a large bowl and set aside.

2 Place the tomatoes in a bowl, cover with boiling water and leave for 30 seconds. Remove from the bowl, peel off the skins, then deseed and chop the flesh. Reserve a little chopped tomato and cucumber for the garnish. Place the rest of the tomatoes and cucumber in the food processor with the peppers, garlic and seasoning, then blend to a purée. Alternatively, use a hand blender.

3 Add the tomato mixture to the avocado purée, mixing thoroughly. Cover and refrigerate for 1 hour, then serve garnished with chives and the reserved tomato and cucumber.

Serves 4

CUMIN-SPICED CARROT SOUP

Ingredients

1 tbsp olive oil
1 large onion, chopped
1 clove garlic, crushed
3 sticks celery, chopped

1 tbsp ground cumin
700g carrots, thinly sliced
900mL vegetable stock
black pepper
fresh coriander to garnish

Method

1 Heat the oil in a large saucepan, add the onion, garlic and celery and fry gently for 5 minutes or until softened, stirring occasionally. Add the cumin and fry, stirring, for 1 minute to release its flavour.

2 Add the carrots, stock and black pepper to the onion mixture and stir to combine. Bring to the boil and simmer, covered but stirring occasionally, for 30–35 minutes, until the vegetables are tender.

3 Remove the pan from the heat and cool for a few minutes. Purée the soup until smooth in a food processor, liquidiser, or with a hand blender. Return to a clean pan and reheat gently. Serve garnished with fresh coriander.

Serves 4

SPINACH AND NUTMEG SOUP WITH CHEESE TOASTS

Ingredients

2 tbsp olive oil

25g butter

250g floury potatoes, such as King
   Edward, peeled and cut into
   2.5cm cubes

250g bag spinach leaves

1 tsp freshly grated nutmeg

1.4 litres chicken or vegetable stock

salt and black pepper

4 tbsp crème fraîche

100g Gruyère, Caerphilly or Cheddar,
   grated

1 large egg, beaten

day-old narrow French bread stick,
cut diagonally into 18 x 1cm slices

Method

1 Heat the oil and half the butter in a large saucepan. Fry the potatoes for 1 minute, then add the spinach and the nutmeg. Cook for 2 minutes or until the spinach is wilting.

2 Add the stock to the potato and spinach mixture, season lightly and bring to the boil. Reduce the heat, cover and simmer for 10–15 minutes, until the potatoes are tender. Leave to cool for 10 minutes.

3 Pour the soup into a food processor and blend until smooth. Alternatively, use a hand blender. Stir in half the crème fraîche, then adjust the seasoning to taste. Set aside.

4 Preheat the grill. Mix the grated cheese with the egg and the rest of the crème fraîche. Lightly toast the bread slices, then spread the cheese mixture over one side of each slice. Dot with the rest of the butter and season with a little black pepper. Grill for 5 minutes or until bubbling and golden. Heat the soup through and serve topped with the cheese toasts.

Serves 6

MIXED VEGETABLE AND BEAN SOUP

Ingredients

2 tbsp olive oil

1 onion, finely chopped

2 cloves garlic, crushed

1 potato, finely diced

1 carrot, finely diced

2 tsp cumin seeds

900mL vegetable stock

2 sticks celery, finely chopped

1 large courgette, finely chopped

125g fine green beans, cut into
   2.5cm pieces

420g canned butter beans, drained

400g canned chopped tomatoes

black pepper

50g Cheddar, grated

Method

1 Heat the oil in a large heavy-based saucepan, then add the onion, garlic, potato, carrot and cumin seeds. Cook, uncovered, for 5 minutes, stirring from time to time, until the vegetables have softened.

2 Add the stock, celery and courgette and bring to the boil. Cover and simmer for 10 minutes or until the celery and courgette are tender.

3 Stir in the green beans, butter beans, chopped tomatoes and plenty of seasoning. Simmer, uncovered, for 5 minutes or until the green beans are tender. Pour the soup into bowls and top with the grated Cheddar.

Serves 4

COCONUT, SWEET POTATO AND SPINACH SOUP

Ingredients

25g butter
450g sweet potatoes, cut into 1cm dice
1 onion, chopped
2 cloves garlic, crushed
1 tsp grated root ginger
1 tbsp medium curry paste

600mL vegetable stock
200mL coconut milk
juice of 1 lime
$^1/_4$ tsp dried crushed chillies
175g fresh spinach, shredded
salt and black pepper

Method

1 Melt the butter in a saucepan and fry the potatoes, onion, garlic, ginger and curry paste for 5 minutes or until lightly golden.

2 Add the stock, coconut milk, lime juice and chilli. Bring to the boil, cover and simmer for 15 minutes or until the potatoes are tender.

3 Leave the soup to cool a little, then purée half of it with a hand blender. Return the purée to the pan, add the spinach and cook for 1–2 minutes, until the spinach has just wilted and the soup has heated through. Season to taste.

Serves 4

INDIAN-SPICED POTATO AND ONION SOUP

Ingredients

1 tbsp vegetable oil
1 onion, finely chopped
1cm piece root ginger, finely chopped
2 large potatoes, cut into 1cm cubes
2 tsp ground cumin
2 tsp ground coriander

$^1/_2$ tsp turmeric
1 tsp ground cinnamon
1 litre chicken stock
salt and black pepper
1 tbsp natural yogurt to garnish

Method

1 Heat the oil in a large saucepan. Fry the onion and ginger for 5 minutes or until softened. Add the potatoes and fry for another minute, stirring often.

2 Mix the cumin, coriander, turmeric and cinnamon with 2 tablespoons of cold water to make a paste. Add to the onion and potato, stirring well, and fry for 1 minute to release the flavours.

3 Add the stock and season to taste. Bring to the boil, then reduce the heat, cover and simmer for 30 minutes or until the potato is tender. Blend until smooth in a food processor or press through a metal sieve. Return to the pan and gently heat through. Garnish with the yogurt and more black pepper.

Serves 4

SPINACH AND ALMOND SOUP

Ingredients

2 x 225g bags baby spinach
600mL vegetable stock
100g ground almonds

salt and black pepper
100mL single cream
50g Parmesan, grated, to serve

Method

1 Put the spinach into a large saucepan with the stock, reserving a few leaves for the garnish. Bring to the boil, then reduce the heat and simmer for 5 minutes. Stir in the ground almonds and seasoning and simmer for 2 minutes. Remove from the heat and leave to cool a little.

2 Pour into a food processor and blend to a smooth purée. Alternatively, use a hand blender. Add the cream, return to the pan and reheat gently – do not let the soup boil. Serve topped with the Parmesan and a sprinkling of black pepper, and garnished with the reserved spinach leaves.

Serves 4

PROVENCAL-STYLE SOUP WITH SPRING ONION PESTO

Ingredients

2 tbsp extra virgin olive oil
1 onion, chopped
1 medium potato, peeled and chopped
1 carrot, chopped
1 yellow pepper, deseeded and chopped
500ml garlic and herb stock, made from
   1½ stock cubes
2 celery sticks, chopped
2 courgettes, chopped

400g can chopped tomatoes
1 tbsp tomato purée
sea salt
freshly ground black pepper
For the pesto
6 spring onions, roughly chopped,
   including green part
50g Parmesan, grated
4 tbsp extra virgin olive oil

Method

1 For the soup, heat the oil in a large heavy-based saucepan, then add the onion, potato, carrot and yellow pepper. Cook uncovered for 5 minutes over a medium heat, stirring occasionally, until the vegetables just start to brown.

2 Add the stock, celery and courgettes and bring to the boil. Cover and simmer for 10 minutes or until the vegetables are tender. Stir in the tomatoes and tomato purée, and season generously. Simmer uncovered for 10 minutes.

3 Meanwhile, make the pesto. Place the spring onions, Parmesan and oil in a food processor and whizz together to a fairly smooth paste. Ladle the soup into bowls and top with a spoonful of the pesto.

Serves 4–6

LEEK, LIME AND COCONUT SOUP

Ingredients

2 tbsp olive oil
3 leeks, thinly sliced
1 green chilli, deseeded and chopped
2 potatoes, diced

grated rind and juice of 2 limes,
  plus a few extra slices to garnish
salt and black pepper
600mL vegetable stock
225mL coconut milk
fresh coriander to garnish

Method

1 Heat the oil in a large heavy-based saucepan, then add the leeks, chilli, potatoes, lime rind and seasoning. Cook for 2 minutes, then add the stock and bring to the boil. Reduce the heat and simmer for 20–25 minutes, until the potatoes are tender. Leave to cool slightly.

2 Transfer the soup to a food processor and blend briefly to make a chunky, creamy mixture. Alternatively use a hand blender. Return the soup to the pan.

3 Stir in the lime juice, then add the coconut milk and heat through, taking care not to let the soup boil. Serve hot or cold, garnished with slices of lime and the coriander.

Serves 4

FRENCH VEGETABLE WITH PISTOU

Ingredients
500g fresh borlotti or dried haricot beans
1 large onion
500g green beans
500g zucchini or patty pan squash
6 medium potatoes
30g butter
3.5mL water
1–2 tsp salt
60g farfalle (pasta bows)

For the pistou
1 cup basil leaves
4 cloves garlic
1 large tomato
1 tbsp tomato paste
1/2 cup grated Parmesan or Gruyère cheese
3 tbsp olive oil

Method

1 If using dried beans, soak overnight. Place soaked and drained dried beans in a pan with fresh water to cover. Bring to the boil, cover and simmer gently for 15 minutes. Drain.

2 Chop onion finely. Trim green beans and cut into short lengths. Trim zucchini or squash into 5mm slices. Peel potatoes and cut into 1cm dice. Melt butter in a large deep pan and sauté prepared vegetables (including dried and cooked or fresh white beans) until softened (about 5 minutes). Cover with cold water and add salt. Cover and simmer gently for 1 hour. Add farfalle to soup, cooking for a further 15 minutes.

3 Make pistou by processing the basil leaves with the garlic in a food processor or blender. Peel and chop the tomato and add to the basil with the tomato paste and grated cheese. Puree to a paste, adding oil gradually. Stir the pistou into the soup just before serving. Serve piping hot with crusty bread.

Serves 4–6

CHILLED YOGHURT SOUP

Ingredients
1 large telegraph cucumber
250mL light single cream
200mL natural yoghurt
2 tbsps white wine vinegar
1 tbsp balsamic vinegar

2 tbsps fresh mint, chopped
1 clove garlic, crushed
salt and freshly ground black pepper
extra mint and slices of cucumber, to garnish.

Method

1 Peel and grate the cucumber.

2 Combine the cream, yoghurt and vinegars together, and whisk lightly, until smooth. Stir in the cucumber, mint, garlic and seasoning. Cover and refrigerate for three hours.

3 Stir and taste for seasoning before serving chilled. Garnish with a slice of cucumber, a sprig of mint and cracked pepper.

Serves 4–6

THICK MINESTRONE WITH PESTO

Ingredients

3 tbsp olive oil

I onion, chopped

2 cloves garlic, chopped

I potato, cut into 1cm cubes

2 small carrots, cut into 1cm cubes

I large courgette, cut into 1cm cubes

1/4 white cabbage, chopped

700mL vegetable stock

800g canned chopped tomatoes

75g pasta shapes, such as shells (conchiglie)

salt and black pepper

4 tbsp grated Parmesan

4 tbsp pesto

Method

1 Place the oil in a large heavy-based saucepan, then add the onion, garlic, potato, carrots, courgette and cabbage and cook for 5–7 minutes, until slightly softened.

2 Add the stock and tomatoes and bring to the boil. Reduce the heat and simmer for 20 minutes, then add the pasta shapes and seasoning and cook for a further 15 minutes or until the pasta is tender but still firm to the bite. Divide the soup between bowls and top each serving with a tablespoon of Parmesan and pesto.

Serves 4

CURRIED CREAM OF VEGETABLE SOUP

Ingredients

3 tbsp groundnut or vegetable oil

2 tbsp curry powder

pinch each of ground cinnamon, nutmeg,
  turmeric and ginger

3 carrots, diced

2 onions, chopped

2 cloves garlic, chopped

2 potatoes, diced

2 courgettes, diced

I litre pints vegetable stock

300g canned cannellini beans, drained

220g canned red kidney beans, drained

200mL crème fraîche

salt

2 tsp chopped fresh flat-leaf parsley
  to garnish

Method

1 Place the oil in a large heavy-based saucepan. Add the curry powder, cinnamon, nutmeg, turmeric and ginger and cook for 1 minute, then add the carrots, onions, garlic, potatoes and courgettes. Stir to coat thoroughly in the oil and spice mixture, and cook for a further 5 minutes.

2 Add the stock and bring to the boil. Reduce the heat and simmer for 20 minutes or until the vegetables are tender. Add the cannellini and red kidney beans and gently heat through. Remove from the heat and stir in the crème fraîche. Season to taste and serve sprinkled with the parsley.

Serves 4

ROASTED PEPPER AND TOMATO SOUP

Ingredients

3 red or orange peppers, halved and deseeded
1 onion, unpeeled and halved
4 large plum tomatoes
4 cloves garlic, unpeeled

350mL chicken or vegetable stock
1 tbsp tomato purée
salt and black pepper
2 tbsp chopped fresh parsley

Method

1 Preheat the oven to 200°C/Gas Mark 6. Place the peppers and onion on a baking sheet, cut-side down, and add the whole tomatoes and garlic. Cook in the oven for 30 minutes or until tender and well browned.

2 Leave the vegetables and garlic to cool for 10 minutes, then peel them. Place the vegetables and garlic in a food processor with half the stock and blend until smooth. Alternatively use a hand blender.

3 Return to the pan, add the remaining stock and the tomato purée, then bring to the boil. Season to taste and scatter with parsley just before serving.

Serves 4

ICED TOMATO SOUP

Ingredients

3 slices bread, crusts removed
1 kg tomatoes, skinned, seeded and chopped or 2 x 425g caned peeled tomato pieces, chopped
1 cucumber, peeled, seeded and chopped
1/2 cup chopped onions
2 cloves garlic, crushed
1/2 green capsicum, seeded and chopped or 1 x 130g canned diced capsicum

1 tsp salt
1 tsp ground cumin
2 tbsps olive oil
2 tbsps wine vinegar
2–3 cups iced water
For the garnish
1 red or green capsicum, diced
1 small cucumber, diced
1 onion, finely chopped
2 hard boiled eggs, chopped
croutons

Method

1 Place all ingredients, except water, into a large bowl and allow to stand for 30 minutes to soften bread and blend flavours.

2 Purée a third of the mixture at a time in an electric blender or food processor. Pour back into a bowl and thin down to desired consistency with iced water.

3 Cover and refrigerate. Adjust seasoning to taste. Serve in chilled bowls or in a large bowl over ice.

4 Place garnish ingredients in separate bowls and allow each diner to add to the soup whatever they like.

Serves 8

CARROT AND LENTIL SOUP

Ingredients
25g butter
1 tbsp sunflower oil
450g carrots, chopped
1 onion, chopped
2 celery sticks, chopped

100g red split lentils, rinsed
850mL vegetable stock
sea salt
freshly ground black pepper
natural yogurt and chopped
fresh parsley, to garnish

Method

1 Melt the butter with the oil in a saucepan and fry the carrots, onion and celery for 6–8 minutes or until lightly golden. Add the lentils and 750mL of vegetable stock and bring to the boil. Cover and simmer for about 20 minutes, until the carrots are tender.

2 Allow the soup to cool for about 15 minutes, then purée until smooth in a liquidiser or food processor. Return to a clean saucepan with the remaining stock, add seasoning to taste and reheat gently before serving. Add a swirl of yoghurt and a sprinkling of chopped fresh parsley, to garnish.

Serves 4

TUSCAN BEAN AND BREAD SOUP

Ingredients

¹/₂ loaf ciabatta
3 tbsp olive oil
3 onions, chopped
3 cloves garlic, chopped

2 x 400g canned chopped tomatoes
400g can flageolet beans
600mL vegetable stock
salt and black pepper
fresh basil to garnish

Method

1 Preheat the oven to 150°C/Gas Mark 2. Cut the ciabatta into dice, then place in the oven for 10 minutes to dry out.

2 Heat the olive oil in a large saucepan, add the onions and garlic, and cook for 3–4 minutes, until soft. Add the tomatoes, beans and stock, bring to the boil, then simmer for 2 minutes.

3 Stir in the diced ciabatta, bring the soup back to the boil, then simmer for a further 5 minutes. Season, then serve garnished with basil.

Serves 4

CREAM OF MUSHROOM SOUP WITH CRISPY ONIONS

Ingredients
25g butter
1 tbsp extra virgin olive oil
4 spring onions, chopped
2 x 200g punnets mushrooms, chopped
1 medium potato, peeled and chopped
850mL vegetable stock
sea salt
freshly ground black pepper
4 tbsp extra thick cream
juice of 1/2 lemon
chopped fresh parsley, to garnish
For the onions
sunflower oil, for frying
1 large onion, finely sliced into rings
1 tbsp white plain flour

Method

1 Heat the butter and oil in a large saucepan and fry the spring onions and mushrooms over a medium to high heat for 5 minutes, until softened and most of the juices have been evaporated.

2 Add the potato, vegetable stock and seasoning and bring to the boil. Reduce the heat, cover and simmer for 20 minutes until the potatoes are tender. Allow to cool.

3 Meanwhile, prepare the onions, heat about 1cm oil in a frying pan. Coat the onions in the flour, add to the pan and cook for 5 minutes or until crisp and lightly golden. Drain on kitchen paper.

4 Purée the soup in a liquidiser or food processor and return to the saucepan, stir in the cream and lemon juice and gently reheat. Ladle the soup into bowls and top with the crispy onions. Sprinkle with chopped fresh parsley, to garnish.

Serves 4

CABBAGE PARCELS IN SOUP

Ingredients
24 cabbage leaves
6 spring onions
4 tbsps coriander, finely chopped
1/2 cup prawns, minced
black pepper
6 1/4 cups vegetable or chicken stock
2 1/2 tbsps fish sauce

Method

1 Blanch cabbage leaves in boiling water and cut away any tough sections from their bases.

2 Cut white ends from spring onions and finely chop the four white heads. Slice two for garnish. Lengthwise, halve green stalks into strips.

3 Mix well the chopped spring onions and 2 tablespoons of the coriander and prawns. Season with pepper.

4 Into each cabbage leaf, place a tablespoon of mixture and fold first the leaf base then outer edges over it and roll up. Carefully tie up each roll with a length of green spring onion then place the parcels gently into boiling stock to cook for 6 minutes.

5 Lift parcels into bowls, pour a cup of stock over each and garnish with remaining sliced spring onions and coriander. Dip rolls into fish sauce when eating.

Serves 6

MIXED-BEAN AND VEGETABLE SOUP

Ingredients

¹/₂ cup haricot beans, soaked overnight
¹/₂ cup chickpeas, soaked overnight
3 tbsps olive oil
1 medium onion, diced
1 clove garlic, crushed
1 leek, white part only; diced
1.5L vegetable stock
2 sticks celery, sliced

1 carrot, diced
2 sprigs fresh thyme, chopped
1 small fennel bulb, grated
2 courgettes, grated
90g broad beans
3 medium tomatoes, peeled, seeded and chopped
salt and freshly ground black pepper
freshly grated Parmesan, for serving

Method

1 Drain the haricot beans and chick peas. Place in a saucepan, cover with water and bring to the boil for 15 minutes. Cover and simmer for a further 30 minutes before draining again.

2 Heat the oil in a saucepan and add the onion, garlic and leek. Continue stirring until tender. Add the stock, haricot beans and chickpeas. Cover, and simmer for 45 minutes (until tender). Add the remaining ingredients, reserving the Parmesan, and simmer for a further 15 minutes.

3 Taste for seasoning, and serve with freshly grated Parmesan.

Serves 4–6

ALMOND SOUP

Ingredients

200g almonds
1 clove garlic, peeled
1 tbsp finely chopped parsley
8 slices stale bread, preferably brown
85mL olive oil

5mL ground cumin
3mL saffron
1L good chicken stock
250mL milk
salt and pepper

Method

1 Fry the almonds, garlic, parsley and four slices of the bread in about 60mL of the oil. When golden, put the contents of the pan in a processor and liquidise with the cumin, saffron and a little of the stock. Put in a saucepan, pour in the remaining stock and the milk, season with salt and pepper, and bring to the boil. Lower the heat and cook slowly for about 15 minutes.

2 Meanwhile, fry the remaining bread slices in the remaining olive oil until golden and crisp.

3 Bring the soup to the boil again and add the four slices of fried bread. Cover, remove from the stove, and leave for 5 minutes before serving.

Serves 4

CHICKPEA, ROASTED TOMATO AND GARLIC SOUP

Ingredients

500g dried chickpeas
1 kg Roma tomatoes
1 bulb garlic
85mL olive oil
salt

2 tbsps dried oregano
2 leeks, sliced, white part only
1L chicken or vegetable stock
2 tbsps tomato paste
salt and pepper
oregano leaves, fresh

Method

1 Soak chickpeas in cold water overnight. Place chickpeas in a saucepan covered with water and bring to the boil, then simmer for approximately one hour until chickpeas are cooked. Drain and set aside.

2 Preheat the oven to 200°C. Halve the tomatoes and place them in a baking tray. Cut the top off the garlic bulb and place in the baking tray.

3 Drizzle with olive oil, sprinkle with salt and dried oregano, and roast in the oven for 20–30 minutes.

4 Place the tomatoes and five peeled garlic cloves (reserve the rest) in a food processor, and purée for one minute.

5 Heat half the remaining oil and sauté the leeks for 3 minutes. Add the stock, and bring to the boil, then reduce heat to simmer. Add the tomato mixture, tomato paste and the chickpeas, season with salt and pepper, and heat through.

6 To serve, sprinkle with fresh oregano leaves just before serving.

Serves 4

salads

MARINATED MUSHROOMS ON A BED OF LEAVES

MARINATED MUSHROOMS ON A BED OF LEAVES

Ingredients

350g mixed mushrooms, such as shiitake, large
  open, button and oyster, thickly sliced
100g baby spinach leaves
25g watercress, thick stems discarded
fresh thyme to garnish

For the dressing
3 tbsp extra virgin olive oil

2 tbsp unsweetened apple juice
2 tsp tarragon white wine vinegar
2 tsp Dijon mustard
1 clove garlic, crushed
1 tbsp mixed chopped fresh herbs; choose
  from oregano, thyme, chives, basil and
  parsley
black pepper

Method

1 To make the dressing, place the oil, apple juice, vinegar, mustard, garlic, herbs and black pepper in a bowl and whisk with a fork to mix thoroughly.

2 Pour the dressing over the mushrooms and stir well. Cover and place in the refrigerate for 2 hours.

3 Arrange the spinach and watercress on serving plates. Spoon the mushrooms and a little of the dressing over the top and toss lightly to mix. Garnish with fresh thyme.

Serves 4

THREE BEAN RICE SALAD

Ingredients

225g brown rice
175g frozen baby broad beans
400g can black-eye beans, drained and rinsed
220g can red kidney beans, drained and rinsed
1 red pepper, deseeded and cut into pieces
1 bunch spring onions, chopped
fresh coriander to garnish

For the dressing
150mL tomato juice
1 tbsp olive oil
1 tbsp white wine vinegar
2 tsp Dijon mustard
1 clove garlic, crushed
2 tbsp chopped fresh coriander
black pepper

Method

1 Cook the rice according to the packet instructions and until tender. Meanwhile, cook the baby broad beans in a saucepan of boiling water for 4–5 minutes, until tender. Rinse under cold water and drain, then remove the skins if you want. Rinse the rice under cold water, drain and place in a salad bowl.

2 To make the dressing, place the tomato juice, olive oil, vinegar, mustard, garlic, coriander and black pepper in a small bowl and whisk together until thoroughly mixed.

3 Pour the dressing over the rice and stir to mix well. Add the broad beans, black-eyed beans, kidney beans, pepper and spring onions and mix well. Cover and refrigerate before serving. Garnish with fresh coriander.

Serves 4

TOMATO AND MOZZARELLA SALAD

Ingredients
6 plum tomatoes, sliced
250g buffalo mozzarella, drained
and sliced
2 spring onions, sliced
75g black olives
salt and black pepper

For the dressing
3 tbsp extra virgin olive oil
1 clove garlic, crushed
2 tsp balsamic vinegar
2 tbsp chopped fresh basil

Method

1 Arrange the tomatoes, mozzarella, spring onions and olives in layers on serving plates and season.

2 To make the dressing, heat the oil and garlic in a small saucepan over a very low heat for 2 minutes or until the garlic has softened but not browned. Remove the pan from the heat, add the vinegar and basil, then pour over the salad.

Serves 4

COURGETTE AND HAZELNUT SALAD

Ingredients
600g small courgettes
2 tbsp sunflower oil, plus extra for frying
5 tbsp walnut oil
1 tbsp white wine vinegar
salt and black pepper

100g bag whole blanched hazelnuts
170g bags watercress, thick stalks removed
75g feta, crumbled

Method

1 Pare the courgettes into lengthwise slivers, using a vegetable peeler. In a bowl, mix together the sunflower oil, walnut oil and vinegar and season. Add half the courgette slivers to the mixture, toss lightly and set aside.

2 Brush a large frying pan with a little sunflower oil and heat. Lay the remaining courgette slivers in the pan and cook for 2 minutes on each side or until lightly charred. Remove, season and set aside. Wipe the pan clean.

3 Roughly crush the hazelnuts, using a pestle and mortar, or put them in a plastic bag, seal it and crush the hazelnuts with a rolling pin. Place in the frying pan and fry for 1–2 minutes, until golden.

4 Divide the watercress between serving plates. Spoon some of the marinated courgettes into the centre, reserving some of the marinade. Scatter over half the toasted hazelnuts and the feta. Arrange the charred courgettes on top, and sprinkle over the rest of the hazelnuts and the reserved marinade.

Serves 6

WARM MEDITERRANEAN PASTA SHELL SALAD

Ingredients
175g dried pasta shells
150g fine green beans, halved
4 spring onions, sliced
1 green pepper, deseeded and chopped
125g cherry tomatoes, halved
1 large ripe avocado, halved, stoned and peeled
black pepper
torn fresh basil leaves to garnish

For the dressing
3 tbsp olive or sunflower oil
1 tbsp white wine vinegar
1 tbsp clear honey
1 tsp Dijon mustard

Method

1 To make the dressing, place the oil, vinegar, honey and mustard in a screw-top jar and shake well to combine.

2 Cook the pasta shells according to the packet instructions. When they are almost cooked, add the green beans and cook for 2 minutes or until the pasta is tender but still firm to the bite and the beans have softened. Drain well.

3 Place the pasta and beans in a large bowl with the spring onions, green pepper, cherry tomatoes, avocado and seasoning. Add the dressing and toss well. Garnish with the basil.

Serves 4

WALDORF SALAD WITH RED LEICESTER

Ingredients
175g red cabbage, finely shredded
4 sticks celery, sliced
150g **Red Leicester**, cut into 1cm cubes
75g red seedless grapes, halved
2 red-skinned eating apples, cored and chopped
1 romaine lettuce, leaves torn
$^1/_2$ tsp poppy seeds

For the dressing
150g tub natural low-fat yogurt
2 tbsp reduced calorie mayonnaise
1 tsp fresh lemon juice or white wine vinegar
black pepper

Method

1 To make the dressing, mix together the yoghurt, mayonnaise, lemon juice or vinegar and seasoning. In a large bowl, combine the cabbage, celery, Red Leicester, grapes and apples, then toss with the dressing.

2 Divide the lettuce leaves between plates and top with the cabbage and cheese mixture. Sprinkle with poppy seeds before serving.

Serves 4

BEETROOT, PEAR AND BITTER-LEAF SALAD

Ingredients
50g walnut pieces
200g bag mixed salad leaves, including radicchio and frisée
225g cooked beetroot in natural juices, sliced
2 pears, quartered, cored, sliced
40g **Parmesan**
fresh chives to garnish

For the dressing
2 tbsp chopped fresh herbs, including basil, chives, mint and parsley
4 tbsp walnut oil
2 tbsp extra virgin olive oil
1 clove garlic, crushed
2 tsp red wine vinegar
1 tsp clear honey
salt and black pepper

Method

1 Preheat the grill to high. To make the dressing, using a food processor or hand blender, blend the herbs, walnut oil, olive oil, garlic, vinegar and honey until smooth in a food processor or with a hand blender. Season to taste.

2 Place the walnuts on a baking sheet and grill for 2–3 minutes, until golden, turning often. Arrange the leaves, beetroot and pear slices on serving plates. Scatter over the walnuts, then shave over thin slivers of Parmesan, using a vegetable peeler. Spoon the dressing over the salad and garnish with whole chives.

Serves 4

TOMATO AND ONION SALAD WITH FETA DRESSING

Ingredients
4 large slicing tomatoes, thinly sliced
I red onion, thinly sliced
salt and black pepper
2 tbsp chopped fresh basil

For the dressing
75g feta, crumbled
3 tbsp natural yoghurt
2 tbsp extra virgin olive oil
I tbsp white wine vinegar

Method
I Arrange the tomato and onion slices on a large serving plate and season with salt and pepper.

2 In a food processor or using a hand blender, blend the feta, yoghurt, oil and vinegar until smooth. Drizzle the dressing over the tomatoes, then sprinkle with basil.

Serves 6

TORTILLA SALAD MEXICANA

Ingredients
Dressing
I small mango, peeled, pitted, diced
$^1/_2$ cup grapefruit juice
$^1/_4$ cup fresh lime juice
I–2 small red chillies
4 shallots, chopped
30mL vegetable oil
I garlic clove

For the salad
oil for frying
4 corn tortillas, cut into strips
3 cups thinly sliced green cabbage
3 cups thinly sliced iceberg lettuce
I mango, peeled and flesh diced
I cup diced, peeled jicama
I red or purple onion, finely diced
3 red peppers, roasted, peeled and sliced
$^1/_2$ cup shelled pumpkin seeds, toasted
$^1/_2$ bunch coriander, chopped
salt and pepper to taste

Method
I First, make the dressing. Place all the ingredients in a blender or food processor and blend until smooth. Set aside.

2 Next, make the salad. Heat oil in heavy medium saucepan over a medium-high heat.

3 Add a handful of tortilla strips and cook until crisp, about 4 minutes per batch, then remove from the oil and drain on absorbent paper.

4 Combine cabbage, lettuce, mango, jicama, onion, peppers, pumpkin seeds and coriander in a large bowl. Toss with enough dressing to coat, adding salt and pepper to taste. Add the tortilla and serve.

Serves 4

AVOCADO, MANGO AND PAPAYA SALAD

Ingredients
2 ripe avocados
Juice of ¹/₂ lime
2 papayas
50g mixed salad leaves
fresh coriander to garnish

For the dressing
1 ripe mango
1 tbsp rice wine vinegar or
1 tsp white wine vinegar
juice of 1 lime
¹/₂ tsp sesame oil
1cm piece fresh root ginger, finely
  chopped
¹/₂ tsp clear honey

Method

1 To make the dressing, peel the mango, slice the flesh off the stone, then chop roughly. In a food processor, blend to a thin purée with the vinegar, lime juice, oil, ginger and honey. Alternatively, press the mango flesh through a sieve, then mix with the other dressing ingredients.

2 Halve and peel the avocados, discarding the stones, then finely slice lengthwise. Toss in the lime juice to stop them turning brown.

3 Halve the papayas, then scoop out and discard the seeds. Peel and finely slice the flesh. Arrange with the avocado and salad leaves on serving plates. Pour over the dressing and garnish with the coriander.

Serves 4

LETTUCE, AVOCADO AND PEANUT SALAD

Ingredients
2 Little Gem lettuces, leaves
  separated
1 head chicory, leaves separated
2 small ripe avocados, stoned, peeled
  and cut into chunks
3 spring onions, chopped
3 tbsp salted peanuts

For the dressing
1 tbsp lemon juice
1 clove garlic, crushed
3 tbsp olive oil
2 tbsp smooth peanut butter
salt and black pepper

Method

1 To make the dressing, put the lemon juice, garlic, oil and peanut butter into a bowl, combine thoroughly and season.

2 Arrange the lettuce leaves, chicory and avocado in a large shallow dish. Pour over the dressing and sprinkle with spring onions and peanuts.

Serves 4

CELERY, CARROT AND APPLE SALAD WITH TAHINI

Ingredients
3 carrots, grated
1 celery heart, thinly sliced
2 eating apples, peeled, cored and thinly sliced

For the dressing
3 tbsp lemon juice
1 clove garlic, crushed
2 tbsp tahini paste
salt

Method
1 To make the dressing, place the lemon juice, garlic, tahini paste and 3 tablespoons of water in a food processor and blend until smooth. Alternatively, combine with a fork. Season to taste.

2 Toss together the carrots, celery heart and apples and transfer to individual serving bowls. Drizzle over the dressing.

Serves 4

GINGERED ALMOND BROCCOLI SALAD WITH CELLOPHANE NOODLES

Ingredients
Noodles
100g dried cellophane noodles
2 tbsps fish sauce
2 tbsps rice vinegar
2 tbsps mirin (sweet Japanese rice wine)
1 tsp palm or brown sugar
$^1/_2$ cup chopped fresh coriander
For the salad
1 tbsp peanut oil
1 tbsp grated fresh ginger
1 very finely sliced small hot red chilli

4 cloves garlic, minced
4 spring onions, minced
500g broccoli florets, trimmed
10 fresh shiitake mushrooms, sliced
200g baby corn
3 tbsps soy sauce
3 tbsps mirin, extra
2 tbsps rice vinegar
1 cos lettuce, shredded
120g blanched almonds, toasted
coriander, extra, for garnish

Method
1 First, prepare the noodles. Fill a deep jug or bowl with very warm water and soak the cellophane noodles for about 10 minutes or until they are soft and tender. Drain. Mix together the fish sauce, rice vinegar, 2 tablespoons of mirin and sugar then toss through the cellophane noodles. Add the coriander, mix well and set aside. Heat the peanut oil in a wok and add the ginger, chilli, garlic and spring onions and toss thoroughly until the spring onions have wilted (about 3 minutes).

2 Add the broccoli florets and toss well until bright green. Add the mushrooms and corn and continue tossing over a high heat. Add the soy, 3 tablespoons of mirin and rice vinegar and continue cooking for 1 minute. Add the noodles and mix well then remove the pan from the heat.

3 Divide the shredded lettuce among the serving plates then top with the broccoli noodle mixture. Garnish with toasted almonds and fresh, chopped coriander.

Serves 4

SUMMER TABBOULEH

Ingredients

175g bulgar wheat
2 medium eggs
1 red onion, finely chopped
2 cloves garlic, finely chopped
1 red and 1 yellow pepper, cored, deseeded and finely chopped
1 tbsp each chopped fresh parsley, chives and coriander

3 tbsp chopped fresh mint
grated rind and juice of 1 lemon
grated rind and juice of 1 lime
3 tbsp olive oil
salt and black pepper

Method

1 Prepare the bulgar wheat according to the packet instructions, until tender. Meanwhile, bring a saucepan of water to the boil. Add the eggs and boil for 10 minutes. Cool under cold running water, then remove the shells and mash the eggs.

2 Add the onion, garlic, peppers, parsley, chives, coriander, mint, lemon and lime rind and juice, and the oil to the bulgar wheat, then mix well. Season to taste before serving.

Serves 4

TUSCAN PANZANELLA WITH ROASTED TOMATO VINAIGRETTE

Ingredients

600g stale, rustic Italian-style bread (about 1/2 loaf)
2 tbsps olive oil
2 tbsps fresh rosemary, chopped
1 kg assorted tomatoes
1 continental cucumber
1 small Spanish onion
20 kalamata olives
20 basil leaves

4 mint leaves, finely sliced
1 tbsp fresh marjoram
For the dressing
4 small tomatoes
1/2 cup quality olive oil
2 tbsps red wine vinegar
1 tbsp balsamic vinegar
3 cloves garlic
salt and freshly ground pepper

Method

1 Cut the bread into cubes and toss with 2 tablespoons olive oil and the rosemary. Spread out on a baking tray and bake at 200°C for 5 minutes until golden, then cool.

2 To make the dressing, heat a heavy pan and brush the skins of the small tomatoes with a little olive oil. Cook these whole tomatoes in the pan until well blackened all over. Purée with the remaining olive oil, vinegars, garlic and salt and pepper to taste. Set aside.

3 Remove the seeds from the other tomatoes and chop into small chunks. Peel the cucumber and remove the seeds by running a teaspoon along the central seed area. Slice finely. Finely chop the Spanish onion. Remove the stones from the olives by squashing them with the wide blade of a knife.

4 In a mixing bowl, place the bread cubes, tomatoes, cucumber, Spanish onion, olives and torn basil leaves. Add the chopped mint and marjoram. Mix well. Pour the dressing over and toss thoroughly. Allow to sit for 10 minutes then serve.

Serves 4

ROASTED VEGETABLE SALAD

Ingredients
3 **red onions, quartered**
3 **potatoes, scrubbed and cut into wedges**
2 **courgettes, thickly sliced**
2 **yellow peppers, deseeded and thickly sliced**
4 **tomatoes, halved**
2 **tbsp olive oil**

sea salt and freshly ground black pepper
Parmesan shavings (optional)
For the dressing
3 **tbsp extra virgin olive oil**
2 **tbsp clear honey**
1 **tbsp balsamic vinegar**
finely grated rind and juice of $^1/_2$ lemon

Method

1 Preheat the oven to 200°C/Gas Mark 6. Place all the vegetables in a shallow roasting tin, drizzle over the olive oil and season. Shake the tray gently to ensure the vegetables are well coated with the oil and seasoning. Bake for about 35 minutes, until the vegetables are really tender and slightly charred at the edges.

2 Meanwhile, mix all the dressing ingredients together and pour over the roasted vegetables. Toss dressing well and divide onto four plates, then top with the Parmesan shavings, if using.

Serves 4

TOMATO AND BREAD SALAD WITH PESTO DRESSING

Ingredients

1 French bread baton, cubed

2 tbsp olive oil

3 large tomatoes, cut into 2.5cm chunks

1 small red onion, thinly sliced

100g feta, crumbled

handful of fresh basil leaves, torn

For the dressing

3 tbsp olive oil

1 red chilli, deseeded and finely
   chopped

2 tbsp red pesto

2 tbsp red wine vinegar

salt and black pepper

Method

1 Preheat the grill to high. Toss the bread in the oil to coat evenly and spread out on a baking sheet. Grill for 1–2 minutes, until golden, turning occasionally, then leave to cool for 10 minutes.

2 Meanwhile, make the dressing. Heat the oil in a small saucepan and fry the chilli, stirring, for 1 minute or until softened but not browned. Remove from the heat, leave to cool slightly, then add the pesto and vinegar. Whisk with a fork and season.

3 Mix the toasted bread with the tomatoes, onion, and feta. Scatter the basil over the salad. Spoon over the dressing and toss lightly to combine.

Serves 4

SICILIAN CAULIFLOWER SALAD

Ingredients

1 small cauliflower

25g seedless raisins

20g toasted flaked almonds

2 tbsp chopped fresh flat-leaf parsley

For the dressing

grated rind and juice of 1 small lemon

1/2 tsp ground cinnamon

pinch of cayenne pepper

5 tbsp extra virgin olive oil

2 tsp balsamic vinegar

1 tsp caster sugar

salt and black pepper

Method

1 Cut the cauliflower into small florets and slice the stalk into bite-sized pieces. Cook in lightly salted, boiling water for 2–3 minutes, until softened but still firm to the bite. Drain well.

2 To make the dressing, place the lemon juice in a screw-top jar with the cinnamon, cayenne, oil, vinegar, sugar and seasoning and shake well, or place the ingredients in a bowl and mix with a fork. Pour the dressing over the cauliflower and toss to coat. Leave to cool for 1 hour.

3 Meanwhile, pour enough boiling water over the raisins to cover, then leave for 10 minutes to plump up. Drain and chop roughly. Scatter over the cauliflower with the almonds, lemon rind and parsley and toss lightly.

Serves 4

WARM SPINACH SALAD WITH WALNUTS

Ingredients

225g bulgur wheat
2 yellow peppers, quartered and deseeded
250g pack green beans, halved
2 ripe tomatoes
4 spring onions, sliced
75g brazil nuts, roughly chopped
4 tbsp chopped fresh parsley

sea salt and freshly ground
black pepper
For the dressing
4 tbsp extra virgin olive oil
I tbsp wholegrain mustard
I garlic clove, crushed
I tsp balsamic vinegar
I tsp white wine vinegar

Method

1 Place the bulgur wheat in a bowl and cover with boiling water to about 2cm above the level of the bulgur wheat. Leave to soak for 20 minutes. Meanwhile, preheat the grill to high. Grill the yellow peppers, skin-side up, for 15–20 minutes, until the skin is blistered and blackened all over. Transfer to a plastic bag, seal and leave to cool. When cold enough to handle, remove and discard the charred skins and roughly chop the flesh.

2 Blanch the green beans in boiling water for 3–4 minutes, drain, refresh under cold running water and set aside. Put the tomatoes into a bowl, cover with boiling water and leave for 30 seconds. Peel, deseed, then roughly chop the flesh.

3 Combine the ingredients for the dressing and mix well. Drain the bulgur wheat and transfer to a salad bowl. Add the dressing and toss well. Add the vegetables, spring onions, brazil nuts, parsley and seasoning and toss together gently to mix.

Serves 4

WARM SPINACH SALAD WITH WALNUTS

Ingredients
2 tbsp walnut oil
5 sun-dried tomatoes in oil, drained and chopped
225g bag baby spinach

I red onion, sliced into thin rings
2 tbsp walnut pieces
salt
3 tbsp chopped fresh coriander to garnish

Method

1 Heat the oil in a wok or large heavy-based frying pan. Add the tomatoes, spinach, onion, walnut pieces and salt to taste. Cook for 1 minute or until the spinach begins to wilt, tossing to combine.

2 Transfer the vegetables to a large salad bowl and sprinkle with the coriander to garnish. Serve straight away.

Serves 4

JAPANESE RICE-NOODLE SALAD

Ingredients

250g long, flat rice noodles
1 tsp olive oil
2 tsps freshly grated ginger
1–2 small fresh red chillies, seeded and minced
1 red capsicum, cut into small chunks
6 spring onions, sliced on the diagonal

1/2 bunch coriander
juice of 1 lime
1 tbsp Japanese rice vinegar
1 tbsp soy sauce
2 tbsps vegetable stock
3 tbsps sesame seeds

Method

1 Fill a large jug or bowl with hot water and immerse the rice noodles, allowing them to soak until soft, about 5–10 minutes. Drain and rinse under cold water to refresh them, then place the noodles in a large mixing bowl.

2 Heat the olive oil in a small nonstick pan and add the ginger and chillies and sauté gently for 1–2 minutes. Add the chopped capsicum pieces and raise the heat to medium high and stir-fry the capsicum pieces until they are softened. Add the spring onion slices and continue to cook for a further 2 minutes.

3 Tip the capsicum mixture into the mixing bowl with the noodles and add the coriander, tossing thoroughly.

4 In a small jug, whisk together the lime juice, rice vinegar, soy and stock and toss through the noodles. Sprinkle with the sesame seeds and refrigerate before serving.

Serves 4

CELERIAC AND HERB REMOULADE

Ingredients

2 medium eggs
500g celeriac, grated
2 tbsp olive oil
1 tbsp sesame oil

juice of 1 lemon
3 tbsp chopped fresh parsley
3 tbsp snipped fresh chives
salt and black pepper

Method

1 Bring a saucepan of water to the boil. Add the eggs and boil for 10 minutes. Cool under cold running water, then remove the shells and finely chop the eggs.

2 Place the celeriac and chopped eggs in a large bowl. Mix together the olive oil, sesame oil and lemon juice and pour over the celeriac and eggs. Add the parsley, chives and seasoning, then mix thoroughly.

Serves 4

BABY SPINACH, FETA, ARTICHOKES AND WALNUT SALAD

Ingredients

1 red capsicum (pepper), quartered
and seeded
20mL olive oil
100g walnuts
200g baby spinach, washed
200g Greek feta, cubed
300g artichoke hearts, quartered

½ cup black olives, pitted
pita bread, for serving

For the dressing
125mL extra virgin olive oil
65mL lemon juice
2 tsps honey
2 tsps oregano, chopped
freshly ground black pepper

Method

1 Preheat grill. Place capsicum under grill, and cook until it turns black on top. Cut into strips and set aside.

2 In a small jar combine all ingredients for dressing, and shake well.

3 In a frying pan, heat one tablespoon of olive oil, add walnuts, and cook for 1–2 minutes. In a large salad bowl combine baby spinach, feta, artichoke hearts and olives, drizzle dressing over ingredients, and serve with pita bread.

Serves 4–6

VIETNAMESE GREEN PAPAYA SALAD

Ingredients

Salad
750g green papaya
4 spring onions, very finely julienned
half white radish, very finely julienned
12 leaves of Asian mint
12 leaves of Thai basil (or regular
basil)
¼ bunch coriander, leaves only
1 clove garlic, minced
2 tbsps dried shrimp or crushed
peanuts

extra Thai basil and Asian mint
leaves, to garnish

For the dressing
¼ tsp shrimp paste
2 tbsps boiling water
3 tbsps rice vinegar
3 tbsps lime juice
2 tbsps fish sauce
2 tbsps sugar
1 tbsp sweet chilli sauce

Method

1 Finely julienne the papaya and toss with the finely julienned spring onions, white radish, chopped fresh herbs and garlic.

2 To make the dressing, dilute the shrimp paste in 2 tablespoons boiling water, then whisk with all other dressing ingredients. If the sauce is a little too acidic, add a little extra water as required to dilute the flavour to your taste. Continue whisking until the dressing is well mixed.

3 Toss the dressing through the papaya/vegetable mixture, taking care to disperse the dressing thoroughly. Pile on a plate and sprinkle with peanuts or dried shrimp. Garnish with Thai basil and Asian mint.

Serves 4

ASIAN GINGERED COLESLAW

Ingredients

¹/₂ large curly cabbage, very finely sliced,
  about 5 cups
4 baby bok choy, leaves separated and sliced
8 spring onions, julienned lengthwise
200g canned sliced water chestnuts, drained
2 medium carrots, finely julienned
2 stalks lemongrass, very finely sliced
4 kaffir lime leaves, very finely sliced

For the dressing

2 tbsps low fat mayonnaise
2 tbsps low fat yoghurt
juice of 2 lemons
juice of 1 lime
1 tbsp freshly grated ginger
4 tbsps rice vinegar
salt and pepper to taste

For the garnish

1 bunch of coriander, well washed and
  roughly chopped
¹/₂ cup toasted peanuts or sunflower seeds

Method

1 Finely slice the cabbage and mix in a large bowl with the sliced bok choy, julienned spring onions, water chestnuts, carrots and lemongrass and lime leaves. Toss thoroughly.

2 In a jug, whisk together all the dressing ingredients until smooth and well seasoned then pour over the salad ingredients and toss thoroughly until all the vegetables are coated with the dressing. To serve, mix through the coriander at the last minute and sprinkle with the crushed peanuts or sunflower seeds.

Serves 4

ROASTED BEETROOT SALAD WITH BALSAMIC AND DILL

Ingredients

24 very small beetroots, greens attached
  if possible
1 tbsp olive oil
salt and freshly ground pepper to taste
1 tbsp butter

2 tbsps balsamic vinegar
3 tbsps fresh dill, snipped
100g hazelnuts, roasted and chopped
2 tbsps sour cream or
  yoghurt (optional)
black pepper to taste

Method

1 If your beetroots have their greens attached, remove them and set the greens aside. Wash the beetroots and scrub them until clean. Trim the bottom if necessary but be careful not to cut the beetroot itself.

2 Toss the beetroots and olive oil together then place them in a baking dish. Cover with foil or a lid and roast at 200°C for 30–45 minutes or until tender.

3 Remove the beetroots from the oven and cool then peel the skin away and discard. Cut the beetroots in half lengthwise and add salt and pepper to taste. Meanwhile, wash the greens thoroughly to remove all traces of sand and grit. Heat the butter in a sauté pan and add the greens, tossing for 1 minute until wilted. Remove the beetroot greens and add the balsamic vinegar and bring to the boil, whisking with the butter. Return the peeled beetroots and toss them in the balsamic until it has reduced and leaves a shiny sheen on the beetroots.

4 Transfer the beetroots to a platter or bowl and arrange with the wilted beetroot leaves. Scatter over the dill and roasted hazelnuts, adding small dollops of the sour cream or yoghurt if desired. Add black pepper to taste.

Serves 4

WILD FLOWER MEADOW SALAD

Ingredients

1 medium egg
50g mixed salad leaves
6 baby corn, thinly sliced into rounds
6 cherry tomatoes, halved
40g seedless white grapes
1 small red eating apple, cored and diced
50g Gruyère, thinly sliced and cut into
  leaf shapes

For the dressing

1 tsp Dijon mustard
2 tbsp olive oil
1 tbsp wine vinegar
2 tbsp natural yogurt
black pepper

Method

1 Hard-boil the egg for 10 minutes in a small saucepan of boiling water. Cool under cold running water, peel off the shell, then cut into sixths. Arrange the salad leaves in bowls and scatter over the baby corn, tomatoes, grapes, apple, Gruyère and hard-boiled egg.

2 To make the dressing, mix together the mustard, oil, vinegar, yoghurt and seasoning. Drizzle over the salad.

Serves 2

SUMMER GREENS WITH LIME AND CORIANDER

Ingredients
250g mangetout, topped and tailed
2 bunches of asparagus, cut in half
250g sugar snaps, topped and tailed
250g fresh peas
¹/₂ punnet cherry tomatoes, cut in half

For the dressing
2 tbsps lime juice
3 tbsps chopped coriander
¹/₂ cup olive oil
1 tbsp white wine vinegar

Method

1 Blanch the mangetout, asparagus and sugar snaps in boiling water for 30 seconds, drain and refresh in a bowl of iced cold water. Drain well.

2 Cook peas in boiling water for 5 minutes, or until tender, drain and refresh in iced water. Drain well. Combine all vegetables and cherry tomatoes.

3 For the dressing whisk all ingredients until well combined and toss over vegetables and serve.

Serves 4

WITLOF SALAD WITH APPLES, BLUE CHEESE AND PECANS

Ingredients
5 heads witlof (Belgian endive)
1 Red Delicious apple, cored, quartered, thinly sliced
1 Granny Smith apple
lemon juice
200g young rocket leaves
1 cup coarsely chopped pecans, toasted
100g crumbled blue cheese such as Gorgonzola or Blue Castello

For the dressing
¹/₄ cup olive oil
¹/₄ cup walnut oil
¹/₄ cup sherry wine vinegar
1 large shallot, minced
salt and pepper to taste

Method

1 Cut the witlof in half, lengthwise then lay the witlof cut side down on a board and cut the leaves into thin strips.

2 Thinly slice the unpeeled apples and toss with the lemon juice.

3 Wash the rocket leaves and drain well.

4 Combine witlof strips, apple slices, rocket, toasted pecans and blue cheese in a large bowl.

5 Whisk the oils, vinegar and shallot in small bowl then season to taste with salt and pepper. Drizzle the dressing over the salad and toss thoroughly. Serve immediately.

Serves 4

BROAD BEANS WITH GRILLED HALOUMI AND LEMON

Ingredients

100g haloumi cheese, halved
oil for brushing
250g broad beans*, fresh or frozen
65mL lemon juice

80mL olive oil
salt and ground black pepper
4 rounds pita bread

Method

1 Preheat griller. Slice haloumi cheese very thinly, then brush with olive oil, and grill until starting to brown.

2 Place the broad beans and haloumi in a bowl, and add the lemon juice, olive oil, salt and ground black pepper, and serve. Serve with toasted pita bread.

Serves 4

*Note: If broad beans are large, peel off outer skin.

OVEN-ROASTED TOMATO AND EGGPLANT FANS WITH SUMMER HERBS

Ingredients

3 small eggplants
4–5 Roma tomatoes
2 cloves garlic, minced
1 tbsp olive oil

10 basil leaves
2 tbsps fresh rosemary
60g feta cheese, crumbled
salt and cracked black pepper to taste
extra basil sprigs

Method

1 Preheat the oven to 250°C. Halve the eggplants lengthwise then, with the cut surface resting on a board, cut the eggplant into $^1/_2$ cm slices, beginning the cuts about 2cm from the core end. Turn the eggplant fans over and sprinkle with salt. Allow to rest for 30 minutes then rinse and dry thoroughly.

2 Meanwhile, slice the tomatoes lengthwise. Mix the minced garlic with the olive oil and set aside.

3 When the eggplant fans have been washed and dried, place them on nonstick oven trays and place a slice of tomato in between every 2 slices of eggplant so that you have alternating eggplant and tomato slices. Tear the basil leaves and insert between the tomato and eggplant slices.

4 Brush the garlic oil over the eggplant and sprinkle with finely chopped rosemary. Bake the eggplant fans at 250°C for 15 minutes then remove from the oven. Crumble the feta cheese over the eggplant fans then add salt and cracked black pepper to taste. Return to the oven for a further 5 minutes or until the cheese browns slightly.

5 Garnish with extra basil sprigs and black pepper, drizzle with extra olive oil and serve immediately.

Serves 2

MINTED BARLEY SALAD

Ingredients

1 cup barley quick
4 cups water
$^1/_3$ cup finely chopped parsley
2 tbsp finely chopped mint
1 bunch spring onions (include some of the green tops), chopped finely

2 tomatoes, chopped
1 red or green pepper, finely diced
4 tbsp olive oil
2 tbsp lemon juice
$^1/_2$ tsp salt
freshly ground pepper

Method

1 Sprinkle the barley into a large saucepan of boiling salted water, stirring. Cook until tender, about 15 minutes. Drain in a colander and rinse under running water. Drain thoroughly.

2 Place barley in a bowl with parsley, mint, spring onions, tomatoes and pepper. Mix together the oil, lemon juice, salt and freshly ground pepper. Add to salad, toss to mix. Refrigerate before serving.

Serves 4

ARTICHOKES BRAISED IN WHITE WINE

Ingredients
6 artichokes
50mL olive oil
I small onion, peeled and finely chopped

2 cloves garlic, peeled and finely sliced
200mL white wine or dry sherry
salt
freshly grated nutmeg

Method

I Remove the stalks and outer leaves from the artichokes and wash well. Cut each one into four pieces. Heat the oil in a casserole and gently sauté the onion and garlic for about 4 minutes. Add the artichokes and wine and season with salt and nutmeg. Cook gently until done, from 20–40 minutes, depending on size and type of the artichokes. (Test by pulling a leaf; if done it will come away easily.) If the liquid should reduce too much you can add a little water.

Serves 4

INDIAN CHICKPEA SALAD WITH SPINACH

Ingredients

2 cups dry chickpeas

4 onions

1 tsp whole cloves

4 bay leaves

60mL peanut or olive oil

4 cloves garlic

1 tsp turmeric

2 tsps cumin

2 tsps garam masala

3 tbsps tomato paste

2 red peppers, sliced

4 medium zucchini, sliced on the diagonal

salt and pepper to taste

2 bunches of spinach or 500g baby spinach

Method

1 Pick over the chickpeas and remove any that are discoloured. Place all remaining chickpeas in a large saucepan and cover with cold water. Peel 2 of the onions and chop in half. Place these in the saucepan with the chickpeas. Add the cloves and bay leaves and bring to the boil and simmer for 10 minutes then remove from the heat and cover and allow to 'steep' for 2 hours. Strain the chickpeas discarding the onions, cloves and bay leaves, and reserving some of the soaking water.

2 Chop the remaining 2 onions. Heat the oil and sauté the onions and the minced garlic. Add all the spices and cook briefly to release their fragrance. Add the soaked chickpeas and 2 cups of the soaking water, the tomato paste and the red capsicum strips.

3 Cover and simmer gently for about 20 minutes until the chickpeas soften and the liquid evaporates. Add the zucchini and salt and pepper to taste and stir well then remove from the heat. Allow to cool slightly then fold through the spinach leaves. Cool completely and serve.

Serves 4

CRUNCHY LENTIL SALAD

Ingredients

1 cup brown lentils

1 1/2 cups crunchy fresh small bean sprouts or alfalfa sprouts

1/2 cup coarsely chopped fresh mint leaves

1/2 red onion, finely chopped

1/4 cup fresh orange juice

2 tbsp extra virgin olive oil

1 tbsp balsamic or wine vinegar

1 tsp grated orange rind

1 tsp ground cumin

1 tsp salt

freshly ground black pepper, to taste

Method

1 Bring a saucepan of lightly salted water to a boil, and add the lentils. Reduce the heat and simmer until just tender, about 30 minutes.

2 Drain the lentils, rinse them under cold water, and pat dry. Place them in a salad bowl and add all the remaining ingredients. Toss well to combine. Cover and refrigerate for several hours before serving.

Serves 4–6

ITALIAN EGGPLANT SALAD

Ingredients

1 large eggplant
$1/4$ cup vegetable oil
2 cloves garlic
$1/4$ cup red wine vinegar

$1/3$ cup olive oil
$1/3$ cup chopped parsley
snipped basil leaves or dill to taste
1 red pepper
1 salad onion, finely chopped

Method

1 Cut the eggplant into cubes and fry very gently with the oil in a covered pan until pale golden and tender. Allow to cool in a colander to help drain some of the excess oil. Meanwhile in a food processor purée the garlic with the vinegar, olive oil, parsley, basil or dill and salt and pepper to taste.

2 Toss the eggplant in the dressing in a salad bowl. Meanwhile char the red pepper over a gas flame or under a hot grill until skin is blackened all over. Now scrape away the blackened skin, rinsing frequently in cold water. When all the pepper is peeled, halve, flick out the seeds and cut into large chunks. Canned pepper can be used instead if you like. Add to the salad and scatter with the chopped onion.

Serves 4

AIOLI GARNI

Ingredients

4 cloves fresh garlic
$1/2$ tsp salt
2 egg yolks

$1/2$ tsp French mustard
freshly ground black pepper
lemon juice to taste
$1 1/4$ cups olive oil

Method

1 Peel the garlic and crush with the flat of a knife. Sprinkle with the salt and still using the knife, work to a smooth paste. Mix in a bowl with the egg yolks, mustard, pepper and lemon juice.

2 Using a wooden spoon to beat, add oil drop by drop beating constantly, until a quarter of a cup has been added. Now add oil in a thin stream, beating all the time. The more oil added the thicker the aioli becomes. If the mixture thins and curdles start again. You will then have to place a fresh egg yolk in another bowl and very gradually beat in the curdled mixture to make the aioli thicker.

3 Arrange the food you have prepared to garnish the aioli on a platter or on individual plates with the aioli in one or two bowls to be shared.

Serves 4

PEAR AND WATERCRESS SALAD

Ingredients

125g soft mild goat cheese, mashed
1 tbsp cream
1/4 cup finely chopped watercress leaves
1 tbsp chopped parsley leaves
2 tbsp chopped toasted walnuts
salt and freshly ground pepper

4 ripe pears
juice of 1 lemon
1 bunch watercress, washed
  and dried thoroughly
2 tbsp white wine vinegar
6 tbsp virgin olive oil

Method

1 In a small bowl, blend together the goat's cheese, cream, watercress, parsley and walnuts, adding salt and freshly ground pepper to taste. Refrigerate the mixture.

2 Just before serving, halve the pears and core, using a teaspoon. Sprinkle each hollow with some of the lemon juice. Into each hollow stuff an eighth of the goat's cheese mixture.

3 Cut the pear halves and cheese through into thick wedges. Arrange the watercress sprigs on a serving platter and drizzle with the vinegar and oil. Top with the pear wedges and serve.

Serves 4

MUSHROOM AND MANGETOUT SALAD

Ingredients

250g fresh mushrooms
125g mangetout
1/2 cup mayonnaise
1 tbsp lime or lemon juice

4 tbsp light sour cream
1 tbsp each chopped parsley, chervil
  and snipped chives
salt and freshly ground pepper
extra snipped chives to garnish

Method

1 Slice the mushrooms very finely. String the mangetout, drop into boiling water for about 10 seconds, drain and refresh in cold water. Cut each one into three diagonal pieces.

2 Place the mangetout in a bowl with the mushrooms. In another bowl combine the mayonnaise with the sour cream, herbs. line or lemon juice, salt and pepper. Fold the dressing into the mushrooms. Turn into a serving bowl and garnish with snipped chives.

MUSHROOM, SPINACH AND PARMESAN SALAD

Ingredients

1 bunch English spinach
250g button mushrooms
1 tsp lemon juice or balsamic vinegar

salt and freshly ground black pepper
2 tbsp extra virgin olive oil
60g Parmesan cheese, shaved using a vegetable peeler

Method

1 Wash the spinach thoroughly, tear into bite sized pieces and spin well to dry. If preparing ahead, pack into plastic bags and store in refrigerator until ready, to crisp and chill. Arrange on serving plates.

2 Just before serving, use the slicing blade of a food processor to slice button mushrooms thinly, adding them to a bowl with the lemon juice or vinegar.

3 Toss lightly with salt and pepper and then pile over the spinach leaves. Drizzle salad with virgin olive oil, scatter with Parmesan shavings and season well with pepper.

Serves 4

main meals

TOMATO, MUSTARD AND BRIE TART

Ingredients

175g plain white flour
sea salt
freshly ground black pepper
75g butter, diced
125mL milk
2 medium egg yolks
1 garlic clove, crushed
1 tbsp wholegrain mustard

50g medium/mature **Cheddar**, grated
4 ripe tomatoes, sliced
1 portion Dutch **Brie**, approx. 125g, thinly sliced

For the herb oil

1 tbsp finely shredded fresh basil
1 tbsp finely chopped fresh parsley
1 tbsp finely chopped fresh coriander
2 tbsp extra virgin olive oil

Method

1 Sift the flour and a pinch of sea salt into a bowl, then rub the butter in, using your fingertips, until it resembles fine breadcrumbs. Add 2 tablespoons of cold water and mix to a dough. Cover and refrigerate for 20 minutes. Use the pastry to line a deep 20cm metal flan tin and chill for a further 10 minutes.

2 Preheat the oven to 190°C/Gas Mark 5. Line the pastry with baking paper and baking beans, then bake blind for 10–12 minutes. Carefully remove the paper and beans and bake the pastry for a further 5 minutes. Set aside, then reduce the oven temperature to 180°C/Gas Mark 4.

3 In a jug, beat together the milk, egg yolks and garlic and season to taste. Spread the mustard over the base of the pastry and sprinkle over the Cheddar. Arrange the tomatoes and Brie on top and pour over the egg mixture. Cook for 30–35 minutes, until just set and golden. For the herb oil, mix all the ingredients together and drizzle over the tart. Serve warm.

Serves 4

OLD BANGER

Ingredients

I large potato, cut into Icm slices
I tbsp vegetable oil
¹/₂ onion, chopped
4 vegetarian sausages, halved widthwise
I small parsnip, sliced
I eating apple, peeled, cored and sliced

I small carrot, sliced
I small courgette, sliced
I tbsp tomato purée
200mL vegetable stock
100mL apple juice
black pepper
I tbsp full-fat milk

Method

1 Preheat the oven to 190°C/Gas Mark 5. Boil the potato slices for 10–15 minutes, until just tender, then drain. Meanwhile, heat the oil in a heavy-based frying pan. Add the onion and sausages and fry for 5 minutes or until the onion has softened and the sausages have browned.

2 Add the parsnip, apple, carrot, courgette, tomato purée, vegetable stock and apple juice, then stir well. Season, then transfer to an ovenproof dish. Arrange the potato slices over the top and brush with milk. Cook, covered, for 40 minutes. Raise the heat to 220°C/Gas Mark 7, then uncover and cook for another 20 minutes to brown the potato.

Serves 2

MUSHROOM PIZZA

Ingredients

400g can chopped tomatoes
2 tbsp olive oil
250g mushrooms, wiped and thinly sliced
2 small garlic cloves, peeled and
  finely chopped

salt and black pepper
I tsp dried oregano
2 x 23cm pizza bases
2 tbsp finely grated Parmesan
150g mozzarella, roughly chopped

Method

1 Put the tomatoes into a saucepan and cook over a medium heat for 15–20 minutes, stirring from time to time, until the sauce has reduced and thickened.

2 Meanwhile, preheat the oven to the highest setting – usually 240°C/Gas Mark 9. Put the oil into a frying pan and heat over a medium heat for 1 minute. Add the mushrooms, garlic, salt, pepper and oregano and cook, stirring from time to time, for 7–10 minutes, until tender.

3 Lay the pizza bases side by side on a large baking tray. Pour half of the tomato sauce onto each base and spread to the edges, using the back of a spoon.

4 Scatter half of the cooked mushroom mixture evenly over each pizza. Sprinkle over the Parmesan and scatter the mozzarella on top. Bake for 8–10 minutes, until the mozzarella is golden and the topping is bubbling.

Serves 4

MUSHROOM AND BLACK OLIVE RISOTTO

Ingredients

25g dried porcini mushrooms
3 tbsp olive oil
I onion, chopped
225g large open mushrooms, chopped
250g risotto rice

450mL vegetable stock
2 tbsp black olives,
pitted and roughly chopped
salt and black pepper
2 tbsp black olive paste
fresh Parmesan to serve

Method

1 Cover the porcini with 200mL boiling water, then leave to soak for 20 minutes. Drain, reserving the water, and set aside. Heat the oil in a large heavy-based saucepan, add the onion and fresh mushrooms and fry for 4–5 minutes. Add the rice and stir to coat with the oil. Fry for 1–2 minutes.

2 Add the porcini and the reserved liquid to the rice with 225mL of the vegetable stock and the olives. Simmer, covered but stirring occasionally, for 10 minutes or until the liquid has been absorbed.

3 Stir in 100mL of the stock and cook for 5 minutes, covered, until absorbed. Add the rest of the stock, the seasoning and the olive paste and cook for 5 minutes, uncovered, stirring constantly. Remove from the heat and leave to rest, covered, for 5 minutes. Shave over the Parmesan, using a vegetable peeler, then serve.

Serves 4

MIXED MUSHROOM RISOTTO

Ingredients

2 tbsps butter
500g mixed mushrooms (oyster,
   shiitake, flat, enoki, Swiss), sliced
40mL olive oil
2 cloves garlic, minced
I leek, finely sliced

IL chicken stock
2 cups arborio rice
¹/₂ cup white wine
rind of I lemon, finely grated
¹/₂ cup pecorino cheese, grated
¹/₂ cup Parmesan cheese, grated
2 tbsps parsley, chopped

Method

1 In a pan, heat the butter, add the mushrooms, and cook for a few minutes. Remove from the heat and set aside.

2 Heat the oil in a large heavy-based saucepan, add the garlic and leek, and cook for 5–6 minutes. Meanwhile, place stock in a saucepan and simmer gently.

3 Add the rice to the leek and garlic and stir for 1 minute, to coat the rice. Add the white wine, and cook, until liquid is absorbed. Start adding the stock, a ladle at a time, stirring continuously, until liquid has been absorbed. Continue adding stock a ladle at a time until stock is used and rice is cooked.

4 Stir in mushrooms, lemon rinds, cheese and parsley, and serve immediately.

Serves 6–8

STIR-FRIED VEGETABLES

Ingredients

2 tbsp vegetable or groundnut oil
5cm piece root ginger, peeled, finely chopped
3 cloves garlic, peeled and finely chopped
2 tbsp dry sherry
1 yellow pepper, deseeded and chopped into 2.5cm pieces
1 red pepper, deseeded and chopped into 2.5cm pieces
2 medium carrots, peeled and thinly sliced on the diagonal
350g broccoli, cut into 2.5cm florets and stalks thinly sliced
300g brown cap mushrooms, wiped and thickly sliced
2 tbsp soy sauce
8 spring onions, cut into 1cm diagonal slices

Method

1 Heat a large wok or heavy-based frying pan over a high heat for 1 minute. Add the oil and rotate the wok or pan to coat the base and lower sides.

2 Add the ginger and garlic and fry, stirring, for 30 seconds. Add the sherry and cook for a further 15 seconds. Add the peppers and carrots and continue to stir and fry for 5 minutes or until the vegetables start to soften.

3 Add the broccoli, mushrooms and soy sauce and fry, stirring, for 3 minutes or until all the vegetables are just tender. Add the spring onions and stir-fry for 1 minute. Serve straight away.

Serves 4

RICE AND APRICOT PILAF

Ingredients

3 tbsp oil or butter
1 large onion, finely chopped
1¹/₂ cups rice
3¹/₂ cups hot water
salt and freshly ground pepper
2 tbsp parsley, finely chopped
2 tbsp lemon juice
200g packet dried apricots
2 tbsp seeded raisins
50g almonds, blanched and toasted

Method

1 In a large saucepan heat oil or butter and fry the onion until pale golden in colour. Add the rice and stir 30 seconds to coat with oil.

2 Add the hot water, salt, pepper, parsley and lemon juice. Cover and simmer for 10 minutes.

3 Stir in the apricots (whole), raisins and almonds and simmer for 5 minutes more. Remove from heat and allow to stand, covered, for 5 minutes before serving to plump the rice. Serve hot with a side salad.

Serves 4

SPINACH SOUFFLÉ

Ingredients

450g fresh spinach
25g sunflower spread, plus extra for greasing
1 tbsp finely grated Parmesan
25g plain flour

250mL half-fat milk
4 medium eggs, separated, plus 1 extra egg white
100g half-fat mature Cheddar, finely grated
black pepper
large pinch of ground nutmeg

Method

1 Rinse the spinach, remove any coarse stalks or leaves and place in a large saucepan. Cover and cook over a low heat for 4-5 minutes or until it has wilted. Drain and squeeze out any excess water. Chop roughly and set aside.

2 Preheat the oven to 190°C/Gas Mark 5. Grease a 1.5 litre, 18cm soufflé dish, sprinkle with Parmesan and set aside. Gently heat the sunflower spread, flour and milk in a pan, whisking continuously, until the sauce boils. Simmer for 3 minutes, stirring. Transfer to a large bowl, add the spinach and mix well. Gradually beat in the egg yolks and 75g of the Cheddar, then season with pepper and nutmeg. Whisk the egg whites in a clean dry bowl until stiff (this is easiest with an electric whisk), then fold into the spinach mixture.

3 Spoon the mixture into the prepared dish and sprinkle with the remaining Cheddar. Bake for 30 minutes or until well risen and lightly set.

Serves 4

PASTA QUILLS WITH PEPPERS AND MASCARPONE

Ingredients

2 tbsp olive oil
1 clove garlic, crushed
2 red onions, chopped
1 red, 1 yellow and 1 green pepper, deseeded
  and cut into 1cm pieces

275g dried pasta quills
200g mascarpone
juice of 1/2 lemon
4 tbsp chopped fresh flat-leaf parsley
black pepper
4 tbsp freshly grated Parmesan (optional)

Method

1 Heat the oil in a large frying pan and fry the garlic, onions and peppers for 10 minutes, stirring frequently, or until the vegetables have softened. Meanwhile, cook the pasta according to the packet instructions, and until tender but still firm to the bite.

2 Stir half the mascarpone, the lemon juice, parsley and seasoning into the pepper mixture. Cook for 5 minutes or until the mascarpone melts.

3 Drain the pasta and stir in the remaining mascarpone, then add to the pepper mixture, tossing together well. Serve with a sprinkling of Parmesan, if using.

Serves 4

TORTELLINI WITH TOMATO AND CREAM SAUCE

Ingredients

50g unsalted butter
I small onion, very finely chopped
I stick celery, very finely chopped
400g passata
1/2 tsp caster sugar

150mL crème fraîche
salt and black pepper
2 x 300g packs fresh spinach and
  ricotta tortellini
freshly grated Parmesan to serve

Method

1 Place the butter, onion, celery, passata and sugar in a heavy-based saucepan and bring to the boil. Reduce the heat and simmer, uncovered, for 30 minutes or until the vegetables have softened and the sauce thickened.

2 Spoon in the crème fraîche, season and bring back to the boil, stirring. Simmer for I minute, then add more salt and pepper if necessary.

3 Cook the pasta in plenty of boiling salted water, until tender but still firm to the bite, then drain. Transfer to a warmed serving bowl and pour over the sauce. Serve with Parmesan.

Serves 4

ROASTED VEGETABLE AND BROCCOLI COUSCOUS

Ingredients

4 parsnips, cut into chunks
salt
2 sweet potatoes, cut into chunks
4 turnips, quartered
2 cloves garlic, crushed
5 tbsp olive oil

4 tbsp apple or redcurrant jelly
300g couscous
500g tomatoes, chopped
handful each of chopped fresh parsley, chives
  and basil
juice of I lemon
300g broccoli, cut into florets

Method

1 Preheat the oven to 200°C/Gas Mark 6. Cook the parsnips in a saucepan of boiling salted water for 2 minutes, then drain. Place in a roasting tin with the sweet potatoes, turnips, garlic and 3 tablespoons of oil, turning to coat. Sprinkle with salt, then cook for 30 minutes or until lightly browned.

2 Melt the apple or redcurrant jelly in a pan with 4 tablespoons of water for 2–3 minutes, until it turns syrupy. Turn the vegetables in the tin and carefully cover with the syrup. Return to the oven for 10 minutes or until browned and glossy.

3 Meanwhile, prepare the couscous according to the packet instructions. Heat the rest of the oil in a frying pan and cook the tomatoes for 2–3 minutes, until softened. Add the couscous and heat through, then mix in the herbs and lemon juice. Meanwhile, boil the broccoli florets for 2 minutes or until tender, then drain. Serve the couscous with the roasted vegetables and broccoli arranged on top.

Serves 4

PUMPKIN RISOTTO IN GOLDEN NUGGETS

Ingredients

4–6 golden nugget pumpkins
4–5 cups chicken stock
salt and freshly ground pepper
1 small onion, finely chopped
$^1/_2$ cup grated pumpkin
75g butter
1$^1/_4$ cups arborio rice (Italian
  short grain rice)
3 tbsp freshly grated parmesan

Method

1 Wash the pumpkins, dry them and rub with a little oil. Place on a baking dish and bake in a preheated moderately hot oven 190°C for 40–50 minutes, until tender when pierced with a skewer.

2 Meanwhile cook the risotto. Bring the stock to the boil in a saucepan, season with salt and pepper and leave gently simmering. In another pan cook the chopped onion and grated pumpkin in 60g of the butter until softened. Add the rice, stirring with a wooden spoon for a few minutes, add about half a cup of the simmering stock. Cook the mixture, stirring until the rice has absorbed the stock. Continue adding the stock until the rice is tender and all the stock is used (about 20 minutes). Remove the pan from the heat and stir in the remaining butter and grated Parmesan.

3 Cut a cap off each pumpkin, scoop out the seeds with a spoon and discard. Fill each with the risotto and serve immediately.

Serves 4

RISOTTO WITH BABY SPINACH AND GORGONZOLA

Ingredients
1L chicken stock
2 tbsps olive oil
2 cloves garlic, crushed
1 onion, finely chopped

2 cups arborio rice
125mL white wine
220g baby spinach
220g Gorgonzola cheese, in small pieces
salt and freshly ground pepper

Method

1 Place stock in a saucepan and bring to the boil. Leave simmering.

2 Heat oil in a large saucepan, add garlic and onion, and cook for 5 minutes, or until soft. Add rice, and stir, until well coated.

3 Pour in wine, and cook, until the liquid has been absorbed. Add a ladle of the stock, stir continuously, until the liquid has been absorbed, then add the next ladle of stock. Keep adding stock this way, and stirring, until all the stock is used, and until the rice is cooked, but still a little firm to bite.

4 Add the spinach, cheese and seasonings, stir, and cook, until spinach is just wilted and cheese has melted. Serve immediately.

Serves 6

GLAMORGAN SAUSAGES WITH TOMATO SALAD

Ingredients
100g potato
salt and black pepper
100g white breadcrumbs
150g Lancashire or Caerphilly cheese, grated
1 small leek, finely chopped
$1/4$ tsp dried sage
1 tbsp chopped fresh parsley
pinch of cayenne pepper
1 medium egg, plus 2 egg yolks

3 tbsp plain flour
oil for shallow frying
For the salad
3 tbsp olive oil
2 tsp balsamic vinegar
pinch of brown sugar
150g cherry tomatoes
1 red onion, thinly sliced
5cm piece cucumber, sliced
few fresh basil leaves

Method

1 Cook the potato in boiling salted water for 15–20 minutes, until tender. Drain well, mash, then leave to cool for 15 minutes. Mix the cold mash with half the breadcrumbs, the cheese, leek, sage and parsley. Season with salt, pepper and cayenne. Bind together with the yolks. Using your hands, shape into 12 sausages. Cover and refrigerate for 1 hour.

2 Season the flour. Beat the whole egg. Dip the sausages into the seasoned flour, then into the beaten egg, then coat in the remaining breadcrumbs. Heat 5mm of oil in a large frying pan and fry half the sausages, turning, for 10 minutes or until golden brown. Drain on kitchen towels and keep warm while you cook the rest.

3 Meanwhile, make the salad. Whisk together the oil, vinegar and sugar. Halve the tomatoes and toss in the dressing with the onion, cucumber and basil. Season and serve with the sausages.

Serves 4

FUSILLI WITH EGGPLANT AND TOMATOES

Ingredients

2 medium eggplant
½ cup olive oil
I clove garlic
4 medium tomatoes

salt and pepper
I–2 tbsp chopped basil
2 tbsp grated parmesan
about 300g dried fusilli
freshly ground pepper

Method

I   Peel eggplant and cut into small dice. Pour half the olive oil into a frying pan and add garlic and diced eggplant. Fry gently until tender.

2   Meanwhile, skin the tomatoes, remove seeds and dice the flesh.

3   Pour the remaining oil into the frying pan and add the diced tomatoes. Cook for about 5 minutes and add salt, pepper and basil.

4   Meanwhile cook the fusilli in boiling, salted water for 10–12 minutes until 'al dente', drain. Toss in the eggplant and tomatoes and sprinkle with grated cheese and black pepper, mixing well.

Serves 4–6

POTATO GNOCCHI

Ingredients

I kg old floury potatoes
1¾ cup plain flour

Method

I   Scrub the potatoes and place in a pan with just enough water to cover them. Cover and boil the potatoes until tender without letting them break up. Drain and peel as soon as you can handle them. Mash and rub through a metal sieve using the base of a glass or jar to help.

2   As soon as the puree is cool enough to handle, start beating in the flour, then as the dough stiffens, turn it out to knead on a floured board. Knead until you have a soft and elastic dough.

3   Next, take a handful of the dough, knead lightly using flour to dust your hands and the work surface. Roll dough into a sausage shape. Cut into 2cm slices.

4   Take a large, slim-pronged fork with round edges. A wooden fork is best but difficult to find. Hold it in your left hand with the prongs down. Take a slice of dough and gently press the dough against the prongs with your thumb, letting the gnocchi roll off on to a clean cloth. Repeat with remaining dough. The gnocchi should curl up into crescent-shaped, ribbed shells as they roll off the fork. A simpler alternative, if you are finding this shaping difficult to master, is to press each slice of dough gently around your finger to curve it, using a fork to make the ribbed grooves. The shaping is not just decorative. It serves to thin out the centre of the gnocchi so that they cook evenly, and the grooves serve to trap the flavours of the sauce.

5   Drop the gnocchi (about 20 at a time) into a large pan of boiling salted water. When they are ready they will float to the surface. Cook them just another 10 seconds, then remove with a slotted spoon to a warm dish. Sprinkle them with freshly grated parmesan cheese and pieces of butter and toss lightly. Serve immediately.

Serves 4

NOODLES WITH BROCCOLI AND CARROTS

Ingredients

250g pack stir-fry noodles

3 tbsp vegetable oil

2.5cm fresh root ginger, finely chopped

2 red chillies, deseeded and finely chopped

4 cloves garlic, finely sliced

2 onions, thinly sliced

2 tbsp clear honey

300mL vegetable or chicken stock or white wine

3 tbsp white wine vinegar

600g 5oz broccoli, cut into florets

300g carrots, pared into ribbons with a
  vegetable peeler

snipped fresh chives to garnish

Method

1 Prepare the noodles according to the packet instructions, then drain. Heat the oil in a large wok or heavy-based frying pan, then add the ginger and chillies and stir-fry for 1–2 minutes to soften.

2 Add the garlic and onions and fry for 5–6 minutes, until the onions have browned. Stir in the honey and cook for 6–8 minutes, until the honey starts to caramelise.

3 Add the stock or wine and vinegar to the onion mixture. Bring to the boil, then reduce the heat and simmer, uncovered, for 8 minutes or until the liquid has slightly reduced. Stir in the broccoli and carrots, cover, and simmer for 8–10 minutes or until the vegetables are cooked but still crunchy.

4 Stir in the noodles and mix well. Cook, stirring, for 2–3 minutes until the noodles are hot and most of the liquid has evaporated. Sprinkle over the chives just before serving.

Serves 6

PASTA WITH DOUBLE TOMATO SAUCE

Ingredients

1 tbsp extra virgin olive oil
1 red onion, finely chopped
2 celery sticks, finely chopped
400g canned chopped tomatoes
1 tbsp tomato purée
285mL vegetable stock

225g punnet cherry tomatoes, halved
1 tsp golden sugar
sea salt and freshly ground
black pepper
340g dried pasta, such as gemelli or penne
4 tbsp crème fraîche (optional)

Method

1 Heat the oil in a large, heavy-based saucepan, then add the red onion and celery and cook uncovered for 5 minutes over a medium heat, until the vegetables are tender. Add the chopped tomatoes, tomato purée and stock and bring to the boil. Simmer, uncovered, for 15 minutes, stirring occasionally, until reduced and thickened.

2 Add the cherry tomatoes, and the sugar and season generously, then stir gently for about 3 minutes, until heated through.

3 Meanwhile, cook the pasta according to packet instructions, until tender but still firm to the bite, then drain. Pour the sauce over the pasta, toss gently to avoid breaking the cherry tomatoes and serve with a dollop of crème fraîche, if using.

Serves 4

HARVEST VEGETABLE BAKE

Ingredients

1 onion, sliced
2 leeks, sliced
2 sticks celery, chopped
2 carrots, thinly sliced
1 red pepper, deseeded and sliced
500g mixed root vegetables, such as sweet
  potato, parsnip and turnip, cubed

175g mushrooms, sliced
400g canned chopped tomatoes
6 tbsp dry cider
1 tsp dried thyme
1 tsp dried oregano
black pepper
fresh herbs, such as basil and coriander,
  to garnish

Method

1 Preheat the oven to 180°C/Gas Mark 4. Place the onion, leeks, celery, carrots, pepper, cubed root vegetables and mushrooms in a large ovenproof casserole dish and mix well. Stir in the tomatoes, cider, thyme, oregano and black pepper.

2 Cover and bake in the centre of the oven for 1–1 1/2 hours, until the vegetables are cooked through and tender, stirring once or twice. Garnish with fresh herbs.

Serves 4

PASTA PRIMAVERA

Ingredients
50g butter
225g bag baby spinach
500g fresh peas, shelled
500g broad beans, shelled
salt and black pepper

4 tbsp crème fraîche
I bunch spring onions, finely sliced
2 tbsp finely chopped fresh parsley
75g Parmesan, grated
350g dried penne (pasta quills)

Method

1 Melt the butter in a saucepan, add the spinach, cover, and cook for 5 minutes or until the leaves wilt. Set aside to cool. Cook the peas and beans in a little boiling salted water for 5 minutes or until tender, then drain.

2 Blend the spinach and crème fraîche to a purée in a food processor or with a hand blender. Return the purée to the pan and stir in the peas and beans. Mix in the spring onions and parsley, season and add half the Parmesan. Keep warm over a low heat.

3 Meanwhile, cook the pasta in boiling salted water according to the packet instructions, until tender but still firm to the bite. Drain, then toss with the spinach sauce. Serve with the remaining Parmesan.

Serves 4

SWEETCORN AND MUSHROOM ROULADE

Ingredients
65g butter, plus extra for greasing
125g mushrooms, chopped
65g plain flour
150mL vegetable stock
125g canned or frozen sweetcorn, drained
 or defrosted
175mL milk

4 medium eggs, separated
For the pepper sauce
I red pepper, deseeded and halved
2 tomatoes
150g Greek yogurt
I tbsp chopped fresh coriander
salt and black pepper

Method

1 Preheat the oven to 200°C/Gas Mark 6. To make the sauce, roast the pepper for 20 minutes. Cool for 10 minutes, then skin and chop. Cover the tomatoes with boiling water and leave for 30 seconds. Peel, deseed and chop, then combine with the pepper, yoghurt, coriander and seasoning.

2 Melt 15g butter in a saucepan, then fry the mushrooms for 3–4 minutes. Add 15g flour, stir for 1 minute, then remove from the heat and gradually stir in the stock. Return to the heat and simmer, stirring, for 1–2 minutes, until thickened. Add the sweetcorn and keep warm. Grease a 25 x 30cm swiss-roll tin and line with baking paper.

3 Melt the remaining butter in a pan and stir in the rest of the flour. Cook for 1 minute, then remove from the heat and slowly stir in the milk. Bring to the boil, stirring. Cool slightly, then beat in the egg yolks. Whisk the whites until stiff, then fold into the yolk mixture. Pour into the tin, then cook for 15 minutes or until golden. Turn out and peel off the lining. Spread with the filling, then roll up and serve with the mushroom and corn sauce.

Serves 4

LINGUINE WITH LEEKS AND MUSHROOMS

Ingredients

500g leeks, sliced
275g button mushrooms, sliced
1 bay leaf
40g sunflower spread

40g plain flour
500mL half-fat milk
2 tbsp snipped fresh chives, plus extra to garnish
black pepper
500g pack fresh linguine or tagliatelle

Method

1 Steam the leeks and mushrooms with the bay leaf over a saucepan of boiling water for 10–15 minutes, until tender. Discard the bay leaf and keep the vegetables warm.

2 Melt the sunflower spread in a pan, add the flour and cook gently for 1 minute, stirring. Remove from the heat and gradually add the milk. Return to the heat and bring to the boil, stirring, until thickened. Reduce the heat and simmer for 2 minutes, stirring. Add the vegetables, chives and black pepper and heat through.

3 Meanwhile, cook the pasta according to the packet instructions, and until firm to the bite. Drain and return to the pan, then add the leek and mushroom sauce and toss lightly to mix. Garnish with fresh chives.

Serves 4

GREEN AS GRASS

Ingredients

75g fine green beans, halved widthwise
75g frozen chopped spinach, defrosted
150g dried tagliatelle verde
2 tsp olive oil
knob of butter
1 clove garlic, crushed

3 tbsp crème fraîche
1/2 tsp pesto
2 tbsp freshly grated Parmesan, plus
  extra to sprinkle
black pepper
2 tsp full-fat milk
1 tbsp chopped fresh parsley

Method

1 Boil the green beans in a little water for 5–6 minutes, until cooked but still crunchy. Drain. Squeeze out any excess water from the spinach. Cook the tagliatelle according to the packet instructions, until just firm to the bite, then drain.

2 Meanwhile, heat the oil and butter in a saucepan, add the garlic and cook for 1 minute to soften. Stir in the crème fraîche, pesto, spinach and Parmesan and heat through for 1 minute. Add the beans and heat for a further 1 minute, then season.

3 Add the pasta to the pan, then stir in the milk and most of the parsley. Toss well and heat through. Pile into bowls, sprinkle with Parmesan and garnish with the remaining parsley

Serves 2

POTATO, CHEESE AND ONION PIE

Ingredients

500g pack fresh shortcrust pastry
450g waxy potatoes, such as Charlotte,
  very thinly sliced

1 small onion, very thinly sliced
100g Red Leicester, finely grated
salt and black pepper
142mL carton double cream

Method

1 Preheat the oven to 180°C/Gas Mark 4. Roll out two-thirds of the pastry on a lightly floured work surface and use it to line a 23cm flan dish. Arrange the potatoes in a single layer over the base of the dish, then top with a layer each of the onion and Red Leicester, seasoning well between each layer. Pour over the cream.

2 Roll out the remaining pastry to make a lid. Lightly dampen the edges of the pie with water. Place the pastry lid on top and pinch the edges together to seal well.

3 Bake for 1–1 1/2 hours, until the potatoes and onions are tender. Leave for 10 minutes before serving to allow the cheese to cool slightly.

Serves 4

SPINACH RISOTTO WITH RAISINS AND ALMONDS

Ingredients

1 bunch English spinach
2 tbsp oil
1/2 bunch shallots, chopped
2/3 cup arborio rice

1 3/4 cups hot water
salt and freshly ground black pepper
3 tbsp lemon juice
100g seeded raisins
50g almonds, blanched and toasted

Method

1 Trim roots from the spinach just above the pink tip. Wash in 3–4 changes of cold water. Drain well and chop roughly.

2 Heat oil in a saucepan, add shallots and sauté a little. Add rice and stir until coated with oil and has coloured slightly (about 30 seconds).

3 Add spinach, hot water, salt, pepper and lemon juice. Cover and cook on medium heat for 10 minutes. Remove lid, stir to combine, add raisins, re-cover and cook for 5 minutes more. Turn off heat and stand, covered, for 5 minutes before serving to plump the rice. Sprinkle with almonds.

Serves 3

BEAN, LENTIL AND AUBERGINE MOUSSAKA

Ingredients

75g continental lentils, rinsed and drained
1 aubergine, thinly sliced
2 tbsp olive oil
2 leeks, sliced
2 sticks celery, chopped
2 cloves garlic, crushed
1 yellow pepper, deseeded and diced
400g can chopped tomatoes

5 tbsp dry white wine
2 tbsp tomato purée
400g canned black-eye beans, drained and rinsed
2 tsp dried mixed herbs
black pepper
300g low-fat natural yoghurt
2 medium eggs
25g Parmesan, finely grated
fresh herbs, such as basil, to garnish

Method

1 Add the lentils to a saucepan of boiling water, cover and simmer for 30 minutes or until tender. Drain, rinse, then drain again and set aside.

2 Preheat the oven to 180°C/Gas Mark 4. Meanwhile, cook the aubergine slices in a saucepan of boiling water for 2 minutes. Drain, pat dry with kitchen towels and set aside.

3 Heat the oil in a frying pan, add the leeks, celery, garlic and pepper and cook for 5 minutes or until slightly softened. Add the cooked lentils, tomatoes, wine, tomato purée, beans, mixed herbs and black pepper. Cover and bring to the boil, then simmer for 10 minutes or until the vegetables have softened.

4 Spoon half the bean and lentil mixture into a shallow ovenproof dish and layer over half the aubergine. Repeat. Mix together the yogurt and eggs and pour over the top. Sprinkle over the Parmesan. Cook for 40 minutes or until golden brown and bubbling. Garnish with fresh herbs.

Serves 4

GREEN VEGETABLE STIR FRY WITH SESAME SEEDS

Ingredients

2 tbsp sesame seeds

2 tbsp groundnut oil

1 clove garlic, roughly chopped

2.5cm piece fresh root ginger, finely
  chopped

150g broccoli, cut into very
  small florets

2 courgettes, halved lengthwise and
  finely sliced

170g mangetout

1 tbsp rice wine or medium-dry sherry

1 tbsp dark soy sauce

1 tbsp oyster sauce

Method

1 Heat a wok. Add the sesame seeds and dry-fry for 2 minutes or until golden, shaking the pan frequently. Remove and set aside.

2 Add the oil to the wok, heat for 1 minute, then add the garlic and ginger and stir-fry over a medium heat for 1–2 minutes, until softened. Add the broccoli and stir-fry for a further 2–3 minutes.

3 Add the courgettes and mangetout and stir-fry for 3 minutes. Pour over the rice wine or sherry and sizzle for a minute. Add the soy and oyster sauces, mix well, then stir-fry for 2 minutes. Sprinkle over the toasted sesame seeds just before serving.

Serves 4

MIXED VEGETABLE CHEESE BAKE

Ingredients

1 large butternut squash, peeled,
  deseeded and cut into chunks

salt and black pepper

3 tbsp olive oil

1 large cauliflower, cut into florets

350g mushrooms, sliced

2 tbsp fresh white breadcrumbs

2 tbsp freshly grated Parmesan

For the sauce

25g butter, plus extra for greasing

25g plain flour

pinch of cayenne pepper

300mL full-fat milk

1 tsp English mustard

100g Cheddar, grated

Method

1 Preheat the oven to 200°C/Gas Mark 6. Put the squash into an ovenproof dish, season, then drizzle over half the oil. Roast for 25 minutes, stirring once, until tender. Meanwhile, cook the cauliflower in boiling salted water for 5 minutes or until just tender. Drain, reserving 200mL of the cooking water, then refresh in cold water and set aside. Fry the mushrooms in the remaining oil for 4–5 minutes.

2 To make the sauce, melt the butter in a saucepan and stir in the flour and cayenne pepper. Cook for 2 minutes, then gradually stir in the reserved cooking liquid. Cook for 2–3 minutes, until thick, then gradually stir in the milk. Simmer, stirring, for 10 minutes. Remove from the heat, then stir in the mustard and the cheese, until melted. Season to taste.

3 Reduce the oven temperature to 180°C/Gas Mark 4. Add the cauliflower to the squash, then divide between four individual ovenproof dishes. Scatter over the mushrooms and pour over the sauce. Mix the breadcrumbs and Parmesan, then sprinkle over each dish. Bake for 30–35 minutes.

Serves 4

PASTA WITH ROASTED SQUASH AND SAGE BUTTER

Ingredients

2 tbsp olive oil

2 cloves garlic, chopped

2 tbsp chopped fresh sage plus extra sprigs to
  garnish, or 2 tsp dried sage

1 butternut squash, peeled, deseeded and
  cut into 1cm dice

350g dried pasta quills

salt and black pepper

75g butter

25g pine nut kernels

25g Parmesan, grated

Method

1 Preheat the oven to 230°C/Gas Mark 8. Toss together the oil, garlic, 1 tablespoon of the chopped fresh sage or 1 teaspoon of the dried sage, and the butternut squash. Cook at the top of the oven for 20 minutes or until tender.

2 Meanwhile, cook the pasta in plenty of boiling salted water, according to the packet instructions, until tender but still firm to the bite.

3 Melt the butter in a large frying pan, add the remaining chopped sage or dried sage and fry gently for 2–3 minutes. Meanwhile, heat another frying pan and dry-fry the pine nut kernels for 3–4 minutes over a high heat, until golden.

4 Drain the pasta, reserving 4 tablespoons of the cooking liquid. Add the reserved cooking liquid to the butter, then add the pasta and cooked squash. Toss, then serve sprinkled with the Parmesan, pine nuts and black pepper. Garnish with fresh sage, if using.

Serves 4

CHILLI MUSHROOM STIR-FRY WITH NOODLES

Ingredients

15g dried porcini mushrooms
200g fresh Chinese noodles
2 tbsp sunflower oil
4 cloves garlic, sliced
1 red chilli, deseeded and chopped
2 tsp ready-made ginger purée or finely grated
  fresh ginger

450g mixed fresh mushrooms, quartered
  or sliced
4 spring onions, sliced
4 tbsp sake or dry sherry
4 tbsp dark soy sauce
2 tbsp lemon juice
1 tbsp sugar, or to taste
2 tbsp chopped fresh coriander

Method

1 Cover the dried mushrooms with 75mL of boiling water and soak for 15 minutes or until softened. Strain and reserve the liquid, then slice the mushrooms. Meanwhile, cook the noodles according to the packet instructions, until tender but still firm to the the bite, then drain.

2 Heat the oil in a wok or large frying pan until smoking, then add the garlic, chilli and ginger and stir-fry for 15 seconds or until they release their flavours. Add all the mushrooms and stir-fry for 2 minutes or until softened.

3 Add the spring onions, sake or sherry, soy sauce, lemon juice, sugar, coriander, reserved soaking liquid from the porcini mushrooms and the noodles, and heat for 1–2 minutes, until warmed through.

Serves 4

AUTUMN TWIGS AND LEAVES

Ingredients
For the leaves
**125g pumpkin, peeled and cut
  into chunks**
**1 small yellow pepper, deseeded and cut
  into chunks**
1 small red onion, quartered
4 cherry tomatoes
2 tsp olive oil, plus extra for greasing
1 tsp balsamic vinegar

50g mixed salad leaves
For the 'twigs'
100g ready-rolled puff pastry
25g Cheddar, finely grated
For the dressing
2 tbsp mayonnaise
1/2 tsp wholegrain mustard
1 small clove garlic, crushed
black pepper

Method

1 Preheat the oven to 190°C/Gas Mark 5. Put the pumpkin, pepper, onion and tomatoes into a roasting tin. Sprinkle with the oil and balsamic vinegar and roast in the centre of the oven for 25 minutes or until soft and slightly browned, turning once.

2 Meanwhile, make the twigs. Lay the puff pastry on a floured surface and cut into 1cm strips. Place on a greased baking sheet and sprinkle with the cheese. Bake at the top of the oven for 10 minutes or until crisp and golden.

3 To make the dressing, mix together the mayonnaise, mustard, garlic and seasoning. To serve, arrange the salad leaves and roasted vegetables on small plates. Serve with spoonfuls of the dressing and the cheesy twigs.

Serves 2

CHILLI FRIED RICE

Ingredients
2 tsps vegetable oil
2 fresh red chillies, chopped
1 tbsp Thai red curry paste
2 onions, sliced
1 1/2 cups rice, cooked

**125g snake (yard-long) or green beans,
  chopped**
**125g baby bok choy (Chinese greens),
  blanched**
3 tbsps lime juice
2 tsps Thai fish sauce (nam pla)

Method

1 Heat oil in a wok or frying pan over a high heat, add chillies and curry paste and stir-fry for 1 minute or until fragrant. Add onions and stir-fry for 3 minutes or until soft.

2 Add rice, beans and bok choy to pan and stir-fry for 4 minutes or until rice is heated through. Stir in lime juice and fish sauce.

Serves 4

118

PASTA WITH GOAT'S CHEESE AND ASPARAGUS

Ingredients

1 tbsp sunflower oil
25g butter
2 red onions, thinly sliced
1 garlic clove, finely chopped
sea salt
275g dried pasta, such as penne

250g bunch asparagus, trimmed and cut into small pieces
150g peas, fresh or frozen
2 x 100g packs Welsh goat's cheese, roughly crumbled
350g dried penne (pasta quills)
freshly ground black pepper

Method

1 Heat the oil and butter in a frying pan, and cook the onion over a medium heat for 7 minutes, stirring occasionally. Add the garlic and cook for a further 3 minutes, until the onions are golden and crisp.

2 Meanwhile, bring a large saucepan of salted water to the boil. Add the pasta and cook for 5 minutes, add the asparagus and cook for a further 2 minutes, then add the peas and cook for 2 minutes. When cooked, drain well.

3 Return the pasta and vegetables to the saucepan and gently stir through nearly all of the onions, saving a small amount for garnish. Add the goat's cheese and plenty of freshly ground black pepper and mix together well. Serve topped with the remaining crispy onions.

Serves 4

RICH BEAN AND VEGETABLE STEW

Ingredients

125g dried porcini mushrooms
3 tbsp olive oil
225g large open mushrooms, chopped
2 carrots, finely diced
1 large potato, diced
225g fine green beans, chopped
1/2 tbsp dried thyme

1/2 tbsp dried sage
2 cloves garlic, crushed
300mL red wine
600mL vegetable stock
salt and black pepper
225g frozen broad beans
300g canned cannellini beans
225g canned flageolet beans

Method

1 Cover the porcini with 600mL of boiling water, then soak for 20 minutes. Meanwhile, heat the oil in a large saucepan, then add the fresh mushrooms, carrots, potato and green beans and fry gently for 3–4 minutes, until slightly softened.

2 Add the thyme, sage and garlic, the porcini with their soaking liquid, the red wine, stock and seasoning. Bring to the boil, then simmer, uncovered, for 20 minutes or until the vegetables are tender.

3 Stir in the broad beans and simmer for a further 10 minutes or until tender. Drain and rinse the cannellini and flageolet beans, add to the mixture, then simmer for 2–3 minutes to heat through.

Serves 4

RED ONION, COURGETTE AND TOMATO PIZZA

Ingredients

1 tbsp olive oil, plus extra for greasing
2 small red onions, sliced
1 yellow pepper, deseeded and sliced
2 small courgettes, sliced
1 clove garlic, crushed
225g plain wholemeal flour
2 tsp baking powder
50g sunflower spread

100mL half-fat milk
4 tbsp passata
1 tbsp tomato purée
2 tsp dried mixed herbs
black pepper
3 small plum tomatoes, sliced
100g half-fat mature Cheddar, grated
fresh basil to garnish (optional)

Method

1 Preheat the oven to 220°C/Gas Mark 7. Heat the oil in a saucepan, then add the onions, pepper, courgettes and garlic and cook for 5 minutes or until softened, stirring occasionally. Set aside.

2 Place the flour and baking powder in a bowl, then rub in the sunflower spread. Stir in the milk to form a smooth dough and knead lightly.

3 Roll out the dough on a lightly floured surface to a circle about 25cm wide and place on a greased baking sheet. Mix together the passata, tomato purée, mixed herbs and black pepper and spread over the dough. Top with the onion mixture.

4 Arrange the tomato slices on top and sprinkle with Cheddar. Bake for 25–30 minutes, until the cheese is golden brown and bubbling. Garnish with fresh basil if using.

Serves 4

CLASSIC HERB OMELETTE

Ingredients

2 large eggs
salt and black pepper
15g butter

2 tbsp chopped fresh mixed herbs, such as parsley and chives

Method

1 Crack the eggs into a small bowl, by sharply rapping them on the rim, then season. Mix lightly with a fork for about 20 seconds, until just blended.

2 Place a small nonstick frying pan over a high heat. When the pan is hot, add the butter and tilt the pan until it covers the base.

3 Pour the eggs into the pan, then tilt the pan so that the eggs cover the base and start to set. After about 10 seconds, use a wooden spatula to pull the cooked egg gently from the edge of the pan towards the centre, so that any uncooked egg runs underneath and sets. Continue pulling the edges until all the egg has set (this will take 2–3 minutes).

4 Sprinkle the herbs evenly over the omelette. Then, using the spatula, gently fold the omelette in half. Tilt the pan and slide the omelette onto a plate.

Serves 1

VEGETABLE STIR-FRY WITH NOODLES

Ingredients

250g pack broad ribbon egg noodles
2 tbsp sunflower oil
1 garlic clove, sliced
2 carrots, thinly sliced diagonally
150g green beans, halved
150g broccoli florets
1 red pepper, deseeded and cut into matchsticks
4 spring onions, thinly sliced diagonally

For the sauce

4 tbsp smooth peanut butter
1 tbsp tomato purée
1 tbsp balsamic vinegar
sea salt and freshly ground black pepper
chopped fresh coriander, to garnish
lemon wedges, to serve

Method

1 Cook the noodles according to the packet instructions, then drain well. Meanwhile, make the sauce: mix together the peanut butter, tomato purée, balsamic vinegar and seasoning, with about 4 tablespoons of cold water. Set aside.

2 Heat the oil in a wok or large frying pan until very hot. Add the garlic, carrots and green beans and stir-fry for 2 minutes, until lightly coloured. Add the broccoli and stir-fry for 2–3 minutes or until softened. Add the red pepper and spring onions, then cook for a further 1 minute.

3 Add the sauce, 125mL water and the drained noodles. Combine well and stir-fry for 4–5 minutes or until everything is hot. Garnish with chopped fresh coriander and serve with fresh lemon wedges to squeeze over.

Serves 4

SPINACH AND ROQUEFORT TART

Ingredients

350g shortcrust pastry, defrosted if frozen
250g bag fresh spinach, thick stalks discarded
black pepper
pinch of freshly grated nutmeg
125g Roquefort or other blue cheese, cubed
1 medium egg, beaten
284ml carton single cream

Method

1 Preheat the oven to 200°C/Gas Mark 6. Roll out the pastry on a lightly floured surface and use it to line a 23cm/9in flan dish. Prick the pastry base with a fork and bake for 10 minutes or until lightly golden.

2 Meanwhile, rinse the spinach and place in a saucepan with the water clinging to its leaves. Cook, covered, for 3–4 minutes, until wilted. Drain, leave to cool slightly, then squeeze out the excess water. Spoon into the pastry base and spread with the back of a wooden spoon. Season with pepper and nutmeg, then add the cheese. Mix together the egg and cream and pour over the top.

3 Bake for 30 minutes or until the filling has risen and is golden. Leave to rest for 10 minutes before serving in slices.

Serves 6

CURRIED VEGETABLES

Ingredients

500g small chat potatoes, cut in half

4 tbsp oil

400g onions, peeled and thinly sliced

250g green zucchini, cut in 2cm-thick rounds

250g yellow squash, cut in half

250g stringless beans, topped, tailed and cut in half

3 tbsp butter or ghee

2 tbsp curry paste

2 tbsp raisins

250g red pepper

2 tbsp pistachio nuts

2 tbsp sunflower seeds

Method

1 Boil the potatoes in boiling, salted water until just tender. Drain and set aside. Heat oil in a frying pan, add the onions and toss to coat with oil. Reduce heat, cover and allow to cook on low heat until onions become soft. Remove lid, increase heat and fry, stirring frequently until the onions are well browned. Drain on kitchen paper.

2 Par boil the zucchini, squash and beans in boiling, salted water for 2 minutes. Drain and immediately cover with cold water. Leave 30 seconds, then drain well.

3 Heat butter or ghee in a large frying pan, add curry paste and cook, stirring, until fragrant. Add potatoes, cook, tossing around the pan until brown and crisp. Add par-boiled vegetables, raisins and peppers. Stir-fry to heat through and coat with curry paste. Toss through the pistachio nuts and sunflower seeds. Remove to a serving platter and top with the fried onions. Serve hot.

Serves 4–5

CREAMY PASTA WITH LEEKS AND COURGETTES

Ingredients

275g dried pasta bows or spirals

I large leek, sliced

50g frozen peas

4 tomatoes

25g butter

I clove garlic, crushed

2 courgettes, halved and sliced

200mL carton crème fraîche

I tbsp tomato purée

2 tbsp chopped fresh basil

black pepper

4 tbsp freshly grated Parmesan

Method

1 Cook the pasta shapes according to the packet instructions. When they are almost cooked, add the leek and peas and cook for 2 minutes, until the pasta is cooked and the vegetables have softened. Drain well.

2 Meanwhile, put the tomatoes in a bowl, cover with boiling water and leave for 30 seconds. Peel, deseed, then chop and set aside. Heat the butter in a large frying pan, then add the garlic and courgettes. Fry for 5 minutes, stirring frequently, until lightly golden.

3 Reduce the heat and stir in the crème fraîche and tomato purée. Add the chopped tomatoes, basil and seasoning and simmer for 5 minutes to heat through. Stir the pasta with the leeks and peas into the sauce and serve sprinkled with Parmesan.

Serves 4

LEMON AND BROCCOLI RISOTTO

Ingredients

1 tbsp olive oil
1 onion, chopped
1 clove garlic, crushed
1¹/₂ cups arborio rice
1 cup dry white wine (e.g. sauvignon
  blanc)

4 cups hot chicken stock
120g broccoli florets
30g chopped fresh parsley
finely grated zest and juice of 1 lemon
crushed black peppercorns

Method

1 Heat oil in a large heavy-based saucepan over a medium heat. Add onion and garlic. Cook, stirring, for 1-2 minutes or until onion is translucent.

2 Stir in rice. Cook for 1–2 minutes. Add wine. Cook, stirring, until liquid is absorbed. Add 1 cup chicken stock and cook, stirring occasionally, until liquid is absorbed. Add another 1 cup stock and cook as described above. Continue adding stock 1 cup at a time, until all the stock is used and the rice is tender. Add broccoli 2–3 minutes before end of cooking time.

3 Stir in parsley, lemon zest and juice and black pepper to taste. Remove pan from heat. Cover. Stand for 3 minutes then serve.

Serves 4

STORTINI WITH CREAMY AUBERGINE AND TOMATO

Ingredients

1 aubergine, diced
salt and black pepper
3 tbsp olive oil
1 onion, finely chopped
4 tbsp vegetable stock
300mL passata

1 tbsp sun-dried tomato purée
300g dried stortini pasta with tomato
  and oregano
4 tbsp crème fraîche
100g feta, crumbled
2 tbsp chopped fresh oregano or basil

Method

1 Place the aubergine in a colander and sprinkle with salt. Set aside for 30 minutes, then rinse and pat dry with kitchen towels.

2 Heat 1 tablespoon of the oil in a large heavy-based frying pan. Fry the onion over a low heat for 5 minutes or until softened but not browned, stirring occasionally. Add the remaining oil and stir in the aubergine. Fry over a medium heat, stirring, for 10 minutes or until the aubergine is soft and golden brown. Add the stock, passata, tomato purée and seasoning. Cover and simmer for 5 minutes or until slightly thickened.

3 Meanwhile, cook the pasta according to the packet instructions, and until firm to the bite. Drain well. Stir the crème fraîche into the sauce, then add the pasta and toss gently. Scatter over the feta and oregano or basil.

Serves 4

RISOTTO OF CHINESE AROMATICS

Ingredients

15g black cloud fungus (or chinese dried mushrooms)
1 cup boiling water to soak
1 tbsp olive oil
1 tbsp toasted sesame oil
1 bunch spring onions
2 cloves garlic, minced
1–2 tbsps grated fresh ginger
$1/2$ tsp chopped red chillies
400g arborio rice
200mL light dry white wine
1 tbsp fish sauce
2 tbsp soy sauce, or to taste
1 tbsp Chinese black bean sauce
$1/2$ cup fresh mint, chopped
$1/2$ cup fresh coriander, chopped
800ml vegetable stock, simmering
$1/2$ cup bean shoots
2 tbsp fresh coriander
150g piece tofu, cut into dice
2 tsps toasted sesame oil, extra

Method

1 Soak the black cloud fungus (or dried mushrooms) in boiling hot water for 30 minutes, then drain, saving the soaking liquid to add to the stock. Set aside the mushrooms.

2 Heat the oils in a saucepan, and add the spring onions, garlic, ginger and red chilli. Sauté for 3 minutes until the ginger releases its pungent aroma. Add the rice and stir to coat. Add the wine, fish sauce, soy sauce, black bean sauce and soaked mushrooms and allow absorption. Stir well to distribute the flavours. Strain the mushroom soaking liquid through a piece of muslin or paper towel to remove any sand or grit, and mix with the simmering stock. When the wine has all been absorbed, begin adding the stock, half a cup at a time. Continue adding stock, half a cup at a time and stirring well after each addition. When adding the last quantity of stock, add the bean shoots and herbs.

2 When most of the stock has been absorbed, remove the pan from the heat, garnish with the tofu cubes, fresh coriander and a drizzle of sesame oil if desired. Serve immediately.

Serves 4

SIMPLE KICHADI

Ingredients

1 cup brown rice
$1/2$ cup black-eyed peas
3 cups water
1 tsp salt

Method

1 Add rice and peas to salted boiling water in heavy pot. Cover, turn heat as low as possible, and simmer gently for just under an hour. If you wish, add a diced raw tomato and a handful of chopped parsley or other fresh herbs.

Serves 4–6

TOFU WITH PEACHES AND MANGETOUT

Ingredients

375g tofu

$^1/_2$ cup flour, seasoned with salt and
  pepper

3 tbsp oil

1 large onion, cut into thin rings

1cm ginger root, peeled

1 clove garlic

300g mangetout, topped and tailed

$^1/_3$ cup dry white wine

200g dried peaches

3 tsp soy sauce

2 tsp sugar

2 tsp fresh ginger juice

Method

1 Cut tofu into 6 cubes. Pat dry with kitchen paper. Coat with seasoned flour; shake off excess.

2 Heat oil in a large frying pan and fry onion rings until golden. Remove with slotted spoon or tongs and drain on kitchen paper. To the oil in the pan add the ginger and garlic, fry for 30 seconds to flavour the oil, remove. Add tofu cubes and fry until golden on all sides, turning with tongs. Adjust heat as needed. Remove and drain on kitchen paper; keep hot.

3 Pour the oil from the pan, taking care not to include the flour sediment. Wipe pan clean with kitchen paper. Return about 1 tablespoon of oil to the pan, add mangetout and stir-fry 1 minute or to desired crispness. Remove to a plate. Pour wine into pan and place in the peaches, in a single layer. Simmer 1 minute, turn peaches. Add soy sauce, sugar and ginger juice. Swirl pan to mix. Heat through.

4 Pile mangetout on serving plates. Arrange tofu cubes and peaches on and around mangetout, pour over the sauce and top with onion rings.

Serves 2–3

LEEK AND MUSHROOM PASTIES

Ingredients

40g butter

2 carrots, cut into matchsticks

1 tsp paprika

4 leeks, thinly sliced

2 cloves garlic, thinly sliced

250g brown cap mushrooms, sliced

5 tbsp double cream

1–2 tsp light soy sauce

2 tbsp chopped fresh parsley

lemon juice to taste

salt and black pepper

500g pack puff pastry, defrosted if frozen

1 small egg, beaten

Method

1 Preheat the oven to 200°C/Gas Mark 6. Melt the butter in a frying pan, add the carrots and paprika and fry gently for 5 minutes or until softened. Stir in the leeks and garlic and fry for 2 minutes, then add the mushrooms and fry for 5 minutes, stirring frequently, until the vegetables are tender and any liquid has evaporated.

2 Stir in the cream and soy sauce, then simmer for 2 minutes. Add the parsley and lemon juice and season. Cool for 30 minutes or until completely cold.

3 Roll out the pastry on a lightly floured surface. Cut out 4 x 20cm circles, using a saucer or small plate as a guide. Divide the filling between the circles, then fold the pastry over to form 4 pasties. Seal the pasty edges with a little beaten egg. Pinch with your fingers, then brush the tops with egg. Cook at the top of the oven for 25 minutes or until browned.

Serves 4

SPINACH AND RICOTTA BAKE

Ingredients

1 tbsp olive oil, plus extra for brushing

1 onion, chopped

1 kg bag frozen whole leaf spinach, defrosted

250g tub ricotta

75g pine nut kernels

$1/4$ tsp ground nutmeg

salt and black pepper

6 sheets filo pastry

1–2 tbsp olive oil for brushing

1 beaten egg for glazing

Method

1 Preheat the oven to 200°C/Gas Mark 6. Heat the oil in a heavy-based frying pan, add the onion and fry for 3–4 minutes, until slightly softened.

2 Put the spinach into a colander, press to squeeze out any excess water, then roughly chop. Place in a bowl and add the onion, ricotta, pine nut kernels and nutmeg. Season with salt and plenty of pepper and mix well.

3 Lightly oil a 30 x 25cm ovenproof dish. Add the spinach mixture, pressing down gently to form an even layer. Place a sheet of filo on top, folding to fit the tin, then lightly brush with oil. Repeat with the remaining filo, brushing each sheet with oil before placing the next on top.

4 Mark the top into 6 portions using a sharp knife, then brush with the beaten egg. Cook for 25 minutes or until golden brown.

Serves 6

COURGETTE, PEPPER AND SWEETCORN FRITTATA

Ingredients

2 tbsp olive oil

I onion, chopped

2 cloves garlic, crushed

3 courgettes, sliced

I red and I yellow pepper, deseeded and sliced

125g canned sweetcorn, drained

6 medium eggs

2 tbsp chopped fresh parsley

2 tbsp chopped fresh basil

I tsp cayenne pepper

black pepper

Method

1 Heat the oil in a large heavy-based frying pan with a flameproof handle. Add the onion, garlic, courgettes and peppers, then fry for 10 minutes or until softened and golden. Stir in the sweetcorn.

2 Meanwhile, beat the eggs with the parsley, basil, cayenne pepper and seasoning. Pour the mixture into the pan and cook over a low heat for 10 minutes or until the base is set and golden.

3 While the frittata is cooking, preheat the grill to medium. Place the pan under the grill and cook for 2–3 minutes until the top is golden brown and the frittata is cooked through.

Serves 4

PASTA WITH MUSHROOMS AND GREEN VEGETABLES

Ingredients

500g pasta, such as snails, shells or spirals

salt

300g broccoli, cut into small florets

I bunch asparagus

60g butter

2 cloves garlic, crushed

I cup lightly cooked or frozen peas

400g fresh button or cup mushrooms left whole, halved or sliced thickly

I cup chicken stock or cream

handful fresh basil leaves, coarsely chopped

freshly grated Parmesan cheese

Method

1 Firstly, cook the pasta. Drop it into a large pan of boiling salted water to which a drizzle of oil has been added and cook according to the packet directions until tender but still firm. Drain and refresh under cold water and toss in a little oil. Leave to stand while preparing vegetables. Drop the prepared broccoli into boiling water for about 4 minutes. Drain and refresh under cold water. Set aside. Meanwhile, break the asparagus spears in two lengths, first breaking off the tough ends and discarding them. Drop prepared asparagus into boiling water for 3 minutes, drain, refresh in cold water, drain again and set aside.

2 Melt half the butter in a large sauté pan and cook the garlic gently for a few minutes. Add the mushrooms over a high heat, toss and add the prepared green vegetables and peas. Season with salt and pepper. Add the cream or chicken stock and cook over high heat until cream or stock reduces and thickens. Sprinkle with the basil and toss. Add the remaining butter to the drained pasta in a large saucepan and toss over a low heat until reheated.

3 Add the vegetables, sauce and a little Parmesan cheese and toss again. Turn into a serving bowl and finish with extra Parmesan cheese.

Serves 4

132

BABY VEGETABLE CURRY WITH PEARS

Ingredients

3 tbsp groundnut oil

2 onions, finely chopped

6 cloves garlic, finely chopped

2 pears, peeled, cored and finely chopped

3 tbsp tomato purée

2 tbsp mild curry powder

600mL vegetable stock

salt and black pepper

200g baby carrots

250g broccoli florets

250g baby cauliflower, quartered

3 tbsp chopped fresh coriander

Method

1 Heat the oil in a large, heavy-based saucepan. Add the onions and garlic and fry for 6–8 minutes, until golden. Add the pears and fry for a further 6–8 minutes, until the pears soften and start to brown, stirring and scraping the bottom of the pan occasionally. Add a little water if the mixture becomes too dry.

2 Stir in the tomato purée and curry powder and fry for 1–2 minutes to release the flavours. Add the stock, season and bring to the boil. Reduce the heat and simmer, uncovered, for 15 minutes or until the liquid has slightly reduced.

3 Add the carrots, cover, then simmer for 5 minutes. Add the broccoli and cauliflower, cover the pan, then simmer for a further 10–15 minutes, until the vegetables are tender. Sprinkle with the coriander just before serving.

Serves 6

TORTILLA WITH SWEETCORN AND SUN-DRIED TOMATOES

Ingredients

225g potatoes, thickly sliced

3 tbsp olive oil

3 tbsp canned sweetcorn, drained

4 sun-dried tomatoes in oil, drained and chopped

2 tbsp chopped fresh parsley

6 medium eggs, beaten

salt and black pepper

Method

1 Boil the potatoes for 10 minutes and leave to cool slightly. Heat the oil in a large, flameproof, heavy-based frying pan, add the potato and fry over a high heat for 2–3 minutes, until browned and crisp. Reduce the heat, then stir in the sweetcorn and tomatoes and heat through for 1–2 minutes.

2 Preheat the grill to medium. Add the parsley to the beaten eggs and season, then pour over the vegetables in the frying pan. Cook over a low heat for 3–4 minutes, until the tortilla base is set and lightly browned.

3 Place the pan under the grill for 1–2 minutes, until the top is set and golden. Leave to cool slightly, then cut into 4 wedges and serve with salad.

Serves 4

ASPARAGUS AND LEMON RISOTTO

Ingredients

2 tbsp olive oil

1 onion, chopped

300g risotto rice

200mL white wine

750mL chicken or vegetable stock

100g pack asparagus tips, cut into bite-sized pieces

50g butter

75g Parmesan, grated

salt and black pepper

2 tbsp chopped fresh parsley

finely grated rind of 1 lemon

Method

1 Heat the oil in a large, heavy-based saucepan or frying pan, then add the onion and fry for 3–4 minutes, until golden. Add the rice and stir for 1 minute or until coated with the oil. Stir in the wine and bring to the boil, then reduce the heat and continue stirring for 4–5 minutes, until the wine has been absorbed by the rice.

2 Pour about one-third of the stock into the rice and simmer, stirring constantly for 4–5 minutes, until the stock has been absorbed. Add half the remaining stock and cook, stirring, until absorbed. Add the remaining stock and the asparagus and cook, stirring, for 5 minutes or until the rice and asparagus are tender but still firm to the bite.

3 Add the butter and half the Parmesan and season. Cook, stirring constantly, for 1 minute or until the butter and cheese have melted into the rice. Sprinkle with the remaining Parmesan and the parsley and lemon rind.

Serves 6

MOROCCAN POTATO AND LEMON CASSEROLE

Ingredients

3 tbsp olive oil

2 onions, sliced

3 cloves garlic, chopped

2 red chillies, finely chopped

1 tsp ground cumin

1 tsp ground coriander

900g waxy potatoes, such as Charlotte, cut into 5mm thick slices

grated rind of 1 lemon, and juice of 1 or 2 lemons

900mL vegetable stock

salt and black pepper

4 tbsp sour cream to serve

3 tbsp chopped fresh parsley to garnish

Method

1 Preheat the oven to 200°C/Gas Mark 6. Heat the oil in a flameproof and ovenproof casserole dish. Add the onions, garlic, chillies, cumin and coriander, then gently fry for 1–2 minutes to release their flavours.

2 Stir in the potatoes, lemon rind and juice to taste, then add the stock and seasoning. Bring to the boil, cover, then cook in the oven for 40 minutes or until the vegetables are tender and the liquid has reduced slightly.

3 Transfer to plates and top each serving with a spoonful of sour cream. Sprinkle with fresh parsley to garnish.

Serves 4

VEGETABLE CHILLI BAKE

Ingredients

1 tbsp sunflower oil

1 onion, chopped

1 green pepper, deseeded and diced

2 cloves garlic, finely chopped

1 large green chilli, deseeded and finely chopped

2 tsp ground cumin

1 tsp hot chilli powder

400g canned chopped tomatoes

1 tbsp tomato purée

3 carrots, cubed

175g swede, cubed

175g mushrooms, chopped

3 sticks celery, finely chopped

6 tbsp vegetable stock

black pepper

420g canned red kidney beans, drained and rinsed

fresh coriander to garnish

Method

1 Preheat the oven to 180°C/Gas Mark 4. Heat the oil in a large flameproof and ovenproof casserole dish. Add the onion, green pepper, garlic and green chilli and cook for 5 minutes or until softened, stirring occasionally.

2 Add the cumin and chilli powder and cook, stirring gently for 1 minute to release the flavours. Mix in the tomatoes, tomato purée, carrots, swede, mushrooms, celery, stock and black pepper.

3 Cover and cook in the oven for 45 minutes, stirring once. Add the kidney beans, cover again and cook for a further 15–20 minutes or until all the vegetables are tender. Garnish with fresh coriander.

Serves 4

ASPARAGUS, RICOTTA AND HERB FRITTATA

Ingredients

450g fresh asparagus
12 medium eggs
2 small cloves garlic, crushed
4 tbsp chopped fresh mixed herbs, including
  basil, chives and parsley
salt and black pepper

50g butter
100g ricotta
squeeze of lemon juice
olive oil or truffle oil to drizzle
Parmesan to serve
fresh chives to garnish

Method

1 Preheat the grill to high. Place the asparagus in a grill pan and grill for 10 minutes or until charred and tender, turning once. Keep warm.

2 Meanwhile, whisk together the eggs, garlic, herbs and seasoning. Melt 25g of the butter in an ovenproof frying pan until it starts to foam, then immediately pour in a quarter of the egg mixture and cook for 1–2 minutes, stirring occasionally, until almost set.

3 Place under the preheated grill for 3–4 minutes, until the egg is cooked through and the top of the frittata is set, then transfer to a plate. Keep warm while you make the 3 remaining frittatas, adding more butter when necessary.

4 Arrange a quarter of the asparagus and a quarter of the ricotta over each frittata, squeeze over the lemon juice, season and drizzle with oil. Top with shavings of Parmesan and garnish with fresh chives.

Serves 4

GNOCCHI WITH MASCARPONE AND BLUE CHEESE

Ingredients

400g pack fresh gnocchi
1 tbsp pine nut kernels

125g mascarpone
113g pack Dolcelatte, crumbled
salt and black pepper

Method

1 Cook the gnocchi according to the packet instructions. Drain well, then transfer to a shallow flameproof dish.

2 Preheat the grill to high. Place the pine nut kernels in the grill pan and toast for
2–3 minutes, stirring from time to time, until golden. Keep an eye on them as they can burn quickly.

3 Meanwhile, put the mascarpone and Dolcelatte in a saucepan and warm over a very low heat, stirring, until melted. Season to taste. Spoon over the gnocchi, then grill for 2–3 minutes, until bubbling and golden. Scatter over the pine nut kernels and serve.

Serves 4

BRAISED VEGETABLES WITH A CHEDDAR CRUST

Ingredients

4 tbsp olive oil
25g butter
2 red onions, thinly sliced
1 head celery, thickly sliced
2 large carrots, thickly sliced
2 cloves garlic, crushed
salt and black pepper
4 large open mushrooms, sliced
3 red peppers, deseeded and
  cut into strips
1 tsp each dried oregano and thyme

2 aubergines, thickly sliced
300mL vegetable stock

For the crust

225g plain flour
2 tsp baking powder
75g chilled butter, cubed
75g Cheddar, grated
2 tbsp fresh breadcrumbs
100mL double cream
2 tbsp chopped fresh parsley
1 tsp dried oregano

Method

1 Heat 1 tablespoon of the oil with half the butter in a large frying pan. Add the onions, celery, carrots and garlic. Cook for 10 minutes, stirring often. Season, remove from the pan and set aside.

2 Preheat the oven to 200°C/Gas Mark 6. Heat another tablespoon of oil in the pan, add the mushrooms, peppers, oregano and thyme and cook for 5 minutes, stirring often. Season and add to the other vegetables. Heat the remaining oil and fry the aubergines for 3 minutes, turning once, to brown.

3 Grease a lasagne dish with the rest of the butter. Add the vegetables, pour in the stock and loosely cover with foil. Cook for 40 minutes. Remove the foil, stir and cook for a further 5 minutes or until tender.

4 Meanwhile, make the crust. Sift the flour and baking powder into a bowl. Rub in the butter, until the texture resembles coarse breadcrumbs. Mix in the Cheddar, breadcrumbs, cream, parsley and oregano and season. Increase the oven temperature to 230°C/Gas Mark 8. Spoon the crust mixture over the vegetables. Cook for 20 minutes or until golden. Set aside to rest for 10 minutes before serving.

Serves 6

ROOT VEGETABLE CURRY

Ingredients

1 tbsp olive oil
1 onion, chopped
1 green chilli, deseeded and finely chopped
1 clove garlic, finely chopped
2.5cm piece fresh root ginger, finely chopped
2 tbsp plain flour
2 tsp each ground coriander, ground cumin
  and turmeric

300mL vegetable stock
200mL passata
750g mixed root vegetables, such as potato,
  sweet potato, celeriac and swede, cubed
2 carrots, thinly sliced
black pepper
chopped fresh coriander to garnish

Method

1 Heat the oil in a large saucepan. Add the onion, chilli, garlic and ginger and cook for 5 minutes or until softened, stirring occasionally. Stir in the flour, coriander, cumin and turmeric and cook gently, stirring, for 1 minute to release the flavours.

2 Gradually stir in the stock, then add the passata, cubed root vegetables and the carrots, season with black pepper and mix well.

3 Bring to the boil, stirring, then cover, reduce the heat and simmer for 45 minutes or until the vegetables are tender, stirring occasionally. Garnish with fresh coriander.

Serves 4

SPRING VEGETABLES IN SPICED COCONUT CURRY

Ingredients

1 stalk lemon grass
2 tbsp vegetable oil
1cm piece fresh root ginger, chopped
1 onion, finely chopped
1 clove garlic, finely chopped
1 tsp turmeric
225g new potatoes, cut into 2cm chunks
2 carrots, thickly sliced

400mL canned coconut milk
2 bay leaves
1 red chilli, deseeded and finely chopped
salt
125g pack baby sweetcorn
170g pack fine green beans
2 courgettes, thickly sliced
2 tbsp chopped fresh coriander
  to garnish

Method

1 Peel the outer layer from the lemon grass stalk, then finely chop the lower white bulbous part and discard the fibrous top. Heat the oil in a large, heavy-based saucepan, then fry the lemon grass, ginger, onion and garlic for 5 minutes or until the onion and garlic have softened.

2 Stir in the turmeric, potatoes and carrots, then add the coconut milk, bay leaves, chilli and salt. Bring to the boil, then reduce the heat and simmer, partly covered, for 10 minutes, stirring occasionally.

3 Add the sweetcorn and beans and simmer, partly covered, for 10 minutes. Add the courgettes and cook for a further 10 minutes or until all the vegetables are tender. Remove the bay leaves and garnish with coriander just before serving.

Serves 4

MUSHROOM AND CRANBERRY TART

Ingredients
350g shortcrust pastry, defrosted if frozen
2 tbsp sesame oil
bunch of spring onions, chopped
250g large open mushrooms, finely sliced
125g pack oyster mushrooms, broken into large chunks
150mL dry white wine

100g cranberries, defrosted if frozen
280g tofu
100mL half-fat milk or soya milk
2 medium eggs, lightly beaten
3 tbsp snipped fresh chives
grated rind and juice of $1/2$ lemon
salt and black pepper

Method
1 Preheat the oven to 220°C/Gas Mark 7. Roll out the pastry and use it to line a 25cm flan dish. Line with baking paper, fill with baking beans and cook for 15 minutes. Remove the paper and beans, then cook for another 5–10 minutes, until golden. Set aside. Reduce the temperature to 190°C/Gas Mark 5.

2 Meanwhile, heat the oil in a wok or large, heavy-based frying pan. Add the spring onions and stir-fry for 2–3 minutes, until they start to brown. Add the large open and oyster mushrooms and stir-fry for 3 minutes or until they begin to soften.

3 Pour in the wine and simmer for 6–8 minutes, until reduced slightly. Add all but a handful of the cranberries and boil for 1–2 minutes, until most of the liquid has evaporated and the cranberries start to pop.

4 Blend the tofu, milk and eggs to a smooth purée in a food processor or using a hand blender. Add the chives, lemon rind and juice and seasoning and mix well. Spoon the mushroom mixture into the pastry case and pour over the tofu purée. Scatter with the remaining cranberries. Cook for 35 minutes or until golden and firm.

Serves 6

CAPPELLINI WITH TOMATOES, GARLIC AND BASIL

Ingredients
120mL olive oil
6 cloves garlic, thinly sliced
550g Roma tomatoes, seeded and diced

$1/3$ cup basil, shredded
salt
black pepper, freshly ground
410g cappellini

Method
1 Heat 60mL of the oil in a pan, add the garlic, and cook over a medium heat, until the garlic is slightly browned and golden.

2 Reduce the heat, and add tomatoes, basil, salt and pepper, and cook for 5 minutes (or until tomatoes are just heated through). Cook cappellini pasta in boiling salted water, until al dente. Add remaining oil to the cooked pasta.

3 Serve with tomato mixture over cappellini pasta.

Serves 4–6

COURGETTE AND CHEESE GRATIN

Ingredients

4 large courgettes, sliced diagonally
400g canned chopped tomatoes
2 tbsp shredded fresh basil
sea salt and freshly ground

black pepper
2 x 125g packs Italian mozzarella,
drained and sliced
15g freshly grated Parmesan
1 tbsp extra virgin olive oil

Method

1 Preheat the oven to 200°C/Gas mark 6. Blanch the courgettes in boiling water for about 4 minutes, drain well and then thoroughly dry them using kitchen paper.

2 Drain the canned tomatoes in a sieve to remove all excess liquid. Layer half the courgettes in a shallow, ovenproof dish, spread with half the sieved tomatoes, then sprinkle with half the basil and a little seasoning. Place half of the mozzarella slices on top in an even layer.

3 Repeat the layers once again, sprinkle with Parmesan, drizzle with olive oil and then cook for about 25 . Alternatively, it makes a lovely accompaniment to most chicken dishes.

Serves 4

BUTTER BEAN TART WITH CARAMELISED ONIONS

Ingredients

225g puff pastry, defrosted if frozen
butter for greasing
2 tbsp olive oil
3 onions, sliced
salt and black pepper
1 tsp caster sugar

420g canned butter beans, drained
2 tbsp freshly grated Parmesan
2 tbsp freshly grated Gruyère
3 medium eggs, beaten
5 spring onions, finely chopped
125g crème fraîche

Method

1 Preheat the oven to 220°C/Gas Mark 7. Roll out the pastry on a lightly floured surface and use it to line a greased 20 x 5cm deep tart tin. Refrigerate for 10 minutes.

2 Heat the oil in a heavy-based saucepan, add the onions, salt and sugar and cook over a low heat for 20 minutes or until the onions have caramelised and turned golden. Set aside.

3 Purée the butter beans in a food processor or with a hand blender, or mash with a fork. Transfer to a bowl and stir in the Parmesan, Gruyère, seasoning and eggs. Mix thoroughly, then pour into the pastry case. Bake for 30–35 minutes, until the top has risen and is golden. Leave to cool for 10 minutes. Meanwhile, mix together the spring onions and crème fraîche. Spoon over the tart and top with the caramelised onions.

Serves 6

SPLIT LENTIL DHAL WITH GINGER AND CORIANDER

Ingredients

200g dried split red lentils
1/2 tsp turmeric
I tbsp vegetable oil
Icm piece fresh root ginger, finely chopped
I tsp cumin seeds

I tsp ground coriander
salt and black pepper
4 tbsp chopped fresh coriander, plus extra leaves to garnish
1/2 tsp paprika to garnish

Method

1 Rinse the lentils and drain well, then place in a large saucepan with 850mL of water. Bring to the boil, skimming off any scum, then stir in the turmeric. Reduce the heat and partly cover the pan. Simmer for 30–35 minutes, until thickened, stirring occasionally.

2 Heat the oil in a small frying pan, then add the ginger and cumin seeds and fry for 30 seconds or until the cumin seeds start to pop. Stir in the ground coriander and fry for I minute.

3 Season the lentils with plenty of salt and pepper, then add the toasted spices. Stir in the chopped coriander, mixing well. Transfer to a serving dish and garnish with the paprika and coriander leaves.

Serves 4

PUMPKIN, LEMON AND PARMESAN RISOTTO

Ingredients

IL chicken or vegetable stock
large pinch of saffron threads
2 tbsp olive oil
15g butter
I onion, chopped
I clove garlic, finely chopped
400g arborio rice

I kg pumpkin or butternut squash, deseeded and cut into 2cm pieces
150mL dry white wine
salt and black pepper
grated rind and juice of I lemon
50g Parmesan, grated
1/2 tsp finely chopped fresh rosemary to garnish

Method

1 Heat 300mL of the stock in a saucepan until boiling, then remove the pan from the heat and stir in the saffron threads.

2 Heat the oil and butter in a large heavy-based pan and gently fry the onion and garlic for 4–5 minutes, until softened but not browned. Add the rice and pumpkin or squash to the pan, and stir for 2 minutes or until the rice is coated with oil.

3 Stir in the wine and boil for a few seconds to cook off the alcohol, then pour in the saffron stock. Simmer, stirring constantly, for 5 minutes or until the stock has been absorbed. Add half the remaining stock and cook, stirring, for 10 minutes or until absorbed. Add the remaining stock and cook, stirring, for a further 10 minutes or until the rice is tender but still firm to the bite. Season.

4 Stir the lemon rind and juice and the Parmesan into the risotto, then garnish with rosemary.

Serves 4

BAKED AUBERGINES WITH GRUYÉRE

Ingredients
**2 tbsp olive oil, plus extra for greasing
and brushing
2 aubergines
450g tomatoes, chopped**

**1 tbsp dried oregano
3 cloves garlic, chopped
salt and black pepper
2 tbsp tomato purée
125g Gruyère, thinly sliced**

Method

1 Preheat the oven to 200°C/Gas Mark 6. Lightly grease a baking sheet. Slice the aubergines down the middle lengthwise. Use a knife and spoon to gouge out the flesh, taking care not to pierce the skin. Chop the flesh into chunks.

2 Place the aubergine flesh in a saucepan with the tomatoes, oregano, garlic, oil and seasoning. Cook gently, uncovered, for 5 minutes or until slightly softened, stirring occasionally. Add the tomato purée and cook for 5 minutes or until the mixture has thickened and reduced.

3 Meanwhile, place the aubergine halves on the baking sheet, brush the insides with oil and cook for 10–12 minutes, until almost tender. Fill the aubergines with the tomato mixture, cover with the Gruyère and return to the oven. Cook for 10 minutes or until the cheese has browned.

Serves 4

SABZEE (GREEN HERB SANDWICH)

Ingredients

large handful of tender English spinach leaves
$1/2$ bunch coriander
8 large parsley sprigs
10 large dill sprigs
2 green spring onions

2 tbsp extra virgin olive oil
pinch of salt
2 pita breads
$1/2$ cup plain yoghurt, seasoned with a pinch
  of cayenne

Method

1 Wash the spinach leaves thoroughly and trim away the stalks below the leaves. Wash the herbs thoroughly and remove larger stems. Chop all roughly and toss with onions and just enough oil to barely coat. Cut the pita breads in half and line each half with the yoghurt before stuffing them with the greens. Nothing more is needed, though additional yoghurt could be served on the side for dipping the sandwich into.

Serves 4

side dishes

SWEET POTATO PUREE

Ingredients

750g sweet potatoes, cut into large chunks
3 tbsp full-fat milk
1 clove garlic, crushed

40g half-fat mature Cheddar, finely grated
1 tbsp chopped fresh parsley
1 tbsp snipped fresh chives, plus extra to garnish
black pepper

Method

1 Cook the sweet potatoes in a saucepan of boiling water for 10–15 minutes, until tender. Drain thoroughly, then mash until very smooth.

2 Heat the milk in a saucepan, then add to the potato with the garlic, Cheddar, parsley, chives and black pepper. Beat until smooth and well mixed, then serve hot, garnished with fresh chives.

Serves 4

HERBED CRUSHED POTATOES

Ingredients

salt and black pepper

I kg floury potatoes, such as King
Edward, unpeeled and cut into
quarters

3 tbsp olive oil

I tbsp snipped fresh chives

25g butter, melted

Method

I Bring a large saucepan of lightly salted water to the boil, then cook the
potatoes for 20 minutes or until tender. Drain and peel, then crush with a fork,
drizzling in the oil. Transfer to a dish.

2 Season and scatter over the chives. Drizzle over the butter just before serving.

Serves 6

SPICY GREEN SALAD

Ingredients

salt and black pepper

I kg mixture of broccoli florets, peas,
mangetout, broad beans, asparagus
and fine green beans

400g can chickpeas, drained

I romaine lettuce, cut into ribbons

85g bag watercress, thick
stalks discarded

I avocado, halved, stoned
and thickly sliced

2 tbsp finely chopped fresh mixed
herbs, such as flat-leaf parsley
and coriander

For the dressing

2 tbsp sesame oil

150mL sunflower oil

4 spring onions, finely chopped

2 cloves garlic, crushed

I tsp dried crushed chillies

2 tsp ground coriander

2 tsp ground ginger

juice of 2 lemons

Method

I To make the dressing, heat the sesame oil and 75mL of the sunflower oil in a frying pan   n fry the spring
onions and garlic for I–2 minutes, until soft but not coloured. Add the crushed chillies, cor   der and ginger and
stir-fry for 2–3 minutes to release the flavours, then transfer to a bowl.

2 Bring a large saucepan of salted water to the boil. Add the vegetables and simmer for 3–4 minutes, until
cooked but still crunchy. Drain.

3 In a large bowl, mix the vegetables with the chickpeas. Pour over the spicy dressing, stir, then drizzle over half
the lemon juice and half the remaining sunflower oil. Stir again and season if necessary. Cover and set aside until
needed.

4 Toss the lettuce with the watercress. Season, drizzle with a little lemon juice and oil, then toss lightly. Arrange
with the vegetables in a serving bowl. Brush the avocado with lemon juice to stop it browning, then add to the
salad with the herbs. Drizzle over the remaining lemon juice and oil. Season to taste.

Serves 20

GREEN BEANS WITH WALNUT DRESSING

Ingredients

450g fine green beans
2 tbsp walnut oil
1 tbsp olive oil

1 tbsp white wine vinegar
1 tsp Dijon mustard
black pepper

Method

1 Cook the beans in a saucepan of boiling water for 5–6 minutes, until tender.

2 Meanwhile, put the walnut oil, olive oil, vinegar, mustard and black pepper in a small bowl and mix together thoroughly. Drain the beans and serve hot or cold with the dressing drizzled over.

Serves 4–6

VEGETABLES WITH TOFU

Ingredients

3 cups mixed prepared vegetables -
   choose from 3 or more of these: green
   beans, carrots, zucchini, mushrooms,
   spinach, Chinese or ordinary cabbage,
   mangetout, green peas, bean sprouts,
   mushroom
1 onion
3 sticks celery

1 pepper
250g tofu
3 tbsps peanut oil
2 cloves garlic, sliced
2 tsp grated fresh ginger
soy sauce
1 tsp sesame oil
2 tbsp toasted sesame seeds

Method

1 Trim vegetables and cut the larger ones into bite size diagonal shapes, squares or slices. Peel the onion and slice downward into wedges, then separate into petal shapes. String celery and slice on the diagonal. Remove seeds and ribs from pepper and cut into squares. Dry the tofu on paper towels and cut into bite size squares.

2 Heat the oil gently with the garlic and ginger in a wok or frying pan. When oil is hot, add tofu and sauté until tofu is browned on both sides. Remove with slotted spoon, discard garlic and ginger, and set tofu aside.

3 Add onion, pepper and celery to the pan and sauté on medium heat for 3 minutes. Add each of the longer-cooking vegetables in turn and sauté for a few minutes between additions, tossing every minute or so, then add the fast-cooking vegetables and toss a minute or two longer. Gently stir in tofu, bean sprouts (if using) and heat through.

4 Season with soy sauce to taste, sprinkle with sesame oil and sesame seeds and serve immediately, with a bowl of steaming white or brown boiled rice.

Serves 4

ROASTED SHALLOTS WITH ROSEMARY

Ingredients
600g shallots or pickling onions
2 tbsp olive oil

1–2 tbsp chopped fresh rosemary
black pepper

Method

1 Preheat the oven to 200°C/Gas Mark 6. Place the shallots in a roasting tin, drizzle over the oil, sprinkle with the rosemary and black pepper, then toss to mix well.

2 Cook in the oven, stirring once or twice for 30–40 minutes, until the shallots are tender and golden brown. Serve hot.

Serves 4

CAULIFLOWER CHEESE

Ingredients
salt and black pepper
1 large cauliflower, cut into florets, thick base discarded
For the cheese sauce
50g butter
50g plain flour

1/2 tsp English mustard powder
pinch of cayenne pepper
600mL full-fat milk
125g mature Cheddar cheese, grated

Method

1 Preheat the oven to 220°C/Gas Mark 7. Bring a large saucepan of water to the boil, then add half a teaspoon of salt. Add the cauliflower florets and cook, covered, for 7–10 minutes, until tender. Drain and set aside.

2 To make the sauce, melt the butter in a large heavy-based pan over a low heat. Add the flour, mustard powder and cayenne pepper and stir briskly to form a smooth thick paste. Cook for 2 minutes, stirring all the time.

3 Remove from the heat and add the milk little by little, stirring each time so there are no lumps. Return the pan to the heat, increase the heat to medium and simmer the sauce for 5–7 minutes, until thickened, stirring constantly.

4 Take the pan off the heat again and add 75g of the cheese, stirring until it melts into the sauce. Season with salt and black pepper. Put the cauliflower into an ovenproof dish, pour over the sauce, then sprinkle the remaining cheese on top. Bake for 10–15 minutes, until the top is golden.

Serves 4

ASPARAGUS WITH LEMON SAUCE

Ingredients

2 bundles asparagus, about 550g in total
salt and black pepper

For the sauce

2 medium eggs
2 tbsp chopped pickled cucumber
  or gherkins

1 tsp capers, rinsed, dried and chopped
1 tsp Dijon mustard
5 tbsp olive oil
finely grated rind and juice of ¹/₂ lemon
pinch of caster sugar (optional)
2 tbsp finely chopped fresh parsley
2 tbsp crème fraîche or fromage frais

Method

1 First make the sauce. Place the eggs in a pan of cold water, bring to the boil and cook for 10 minutes or until hard boiled. Peel, halve and remove the yolks, discarding the whites.

2 Mash the yolks in a bowl with the cucumber or gherkins. Stir in the capers and mustard, then gradually beat in the oil. Alternatively, blend in a food processor or with a hand blender. Beat in the lemon rind, juice and sugar, if using, then stir in the parsley and crème fraîche or fromage frais.

3 Cut the tough ends off the asparagus, then peel the lower 5cm using a vegetable peeler. Fill a saucepan with water to a depth of about 4cm, add a little salt, then bring to the boil. Stand the asparagus spears in the pan, keeping the tips out of the water. Simmer for 5–6 minutes, until just tender, then drain. Serve the asparagus with the sauce and grind over black pepper.

Serves 4

CORN COBS WITH MIXED VEGETABLES IN COCONUT MILK

Ingredients

3–4 corn cobs
1 kg mixed vegetables (choose from French beans, potatoes, butternut pumpkin, carrot, cauliflower, okra, etc)
1/2 bunch spinach
small bunch fresh coriander

2.5cm piece fresh green ginger
2 green chillies
2 tbsp oil
2 tsp salt
1 tsp ground coriander
1 tsp cumin
1 can coconut milk

Method

1 Remove the outside leaves and as much of the silk as possible from the corn and cut each cob into four pieces. Peel and cut all the vegetables into chunks or cubes. Remove the white stalks and chop the spinach and coriander. Wash them both and set aside. Place the other vegetables in a colander and wash well. Peel and grate the ginger and seed and chop the chillies.

2 Heat the oil in a large heavy saucepan. Add the ginger and chillies and stir in the corn pieces. Scatter over half the chopped spinach and coriander, spoon in all the vegetables and scatter over the remaining spinach and coriander.

3 Add salt, ground coriander and cumin to the coconut milk and pour half of the milk over the vegetables. Cover with a tight-fitting lid and simmer very gently for 10–15 minutes or until vegetables are cooked but still crisp. Remove the lid and add the remaining coconut cream. Serve immediately. Garnish with fresh coriander.

Serves 4–6

CREAMY POLENTA, SPINACH AND CHEESE BAKE

Ingredients

1 tbsp olive oil
1 small onion, finely chopped
2 cloves garlic, crushed
1/2 tsp ground coriander
3 x 250g bags fresh spinach
284mL single cream

50g Gorgonzola, crumbled
pinch of ground nutmeg
salt and black pepper
500g pack ready-made polenta,
  thinly sliced
150g mozzarella ball, thinly sliced

Method

1 Preheat the oven to 230°C/Gas Mark 8. Heat the oil in a saucepan and gently fry the onion, garlic and coriander for 5 minutes or until the onion is softened.

2 Blanch the spinach in boiling salted water for 1 minute, refresh under cold running water, then drain well and squeeze out any excess moisture. Stir the spinach into the pan with the cream, Gorgonzola, nutmeg, salt and pepper. Bring to a simmer, then transfer to a large, shallow, ovenproof dish.

3 Arrange the polenta and mozzarella slices over the top of the spinach mixture, pressing down well. Bake for 15 minutes or until bubbling. Meanwhile, preheat the grill to high. Place the bake under the grill for 1–2 minutes, until browned.

Serves 4

BAKED ONIONS AND GREEN PEPPERS

Ingredients

4 onions, quartered
3 sprigs of thyme
100mL vegetable or chicken stock
  or white wine
3 tbsp cider vinegar
2 tbsp olive oil

1 tbsp molasses or soft dark
  brown sugar
2 tsp caraway seeds
4 cloves garlic, peeled and left whole
salt and black pepper
3 green peppers, deseeded and cut into
  wide strips

Method

1 Preheat the oven to 200°C/Gas Mark 6. Place the onions, thyme, stock or wine, vinegar, oil, molasses or sugar, caraway seeds and garlic (if using) in an ovenproof dish. Season, cover with foil and bake for 30 minutes or until the onions have softened slightly.

2 Remove the foil, baste the onions with the cooking liquid, then re-cover and return to the oven for 30 minutes or until the onions are just tender. Add a little water if the liquid has evaporated.

3 Increase the oven heat to maximum. Remove the foil from the dish and stir in the pepper strips. Return the dish to the oven, uncovered, and cook the vegetables for 8–10 minutes, turning halfway through cooking, until most of the liquid has evaporated and the vegetables have started to brown.

Serves 6

MANGETOUT AND CARROTS WITH SESAME SEEDS

Ingredients

1/2 cucumber

2 tbsp sesame seeds

1 tbsp sunflower oil

4 carrots, cut into matchsticks

225g mangetout

6 spring onions, chopped

1 tbsp lemon juice

black pepper

Method

1 Peel the cucumber, cut it in half lengthwise and scoop out the seeds. Slice into half moons.

2 Heat a nonstick wok or large frying pan. Add the sesame seeds and dry-fry for
1 minute or until toasted, tossing constantly. Remove and set aside. Add the oil, then the cucumber
and carrots and stir-fry over a high heat for 2 minutes. Add the mangetout and spring onions and
stir-fry for a further 2–3 minutes, until all the vegetables are cooked but still crisp.

3 Sprinkle over the lemon juice and sesame seeds, toss to mix and stir-fry for a few seconds to
heat through. Season with pepper and serve.

Serves 4

AMERICAN POTATO SALAD

Ingredients

1 kg new potatoes

1/3 cup dry white wine

1/2 cup vinaigrette dressing

1 red onion, sliced into rings

1 stalk celery, sliced

2 dill pickles or gherkins, thinly sliced

1 tsp capers

4 hard boiled eggs, peeled and sliced
  chopped parsley

salt and freshly ground pepper

Method

1 Scrub and boil potatoes until tender in salted water. Peel and slice them while still hot and place
them into a bowl. Sprinkle with white wine, turning the potato slices carefully. Now sprinkle with the
vinaigrette dressing and add the remaining ingredients. Season with salt and pepper to serve.

2 Variation with mayonnaise: Follow the recipe and fold in half a cup of mayonnaise or a quarter of a
cup each sour cream and mayonnaise before adding the remaining ingredients. This is easy to do
because the potatoes are by now oil coated, which also means less mayonnaise is needed.

Serves 4

EGGPLANT ROLLS

Ingredients
2 x 225g eggplant
3 tbsp olive oil
3 medium tomatoes, seeded and diced
150g mozzarella cheese, finely diced
2 tbsps fresh basil, chopped
salt and freshly ground black pepper
fresh basil leaves, for serving

For the dressing
¼ cup olive oil
1 tomato, diced
1 tbsp balsamic vinegar
2 tbsps pine nuts, toasted

Method

1   Remove the stalks from eggplants, and slice the eggplants lengthwise thinly to thick 5mm. Brush the slices on both sides with oil, and grill on both sides (until soft and beginning to brown).

2   Preheat the oven to 180°C. Combine together (in a bowl) the tomatoes, mozzarella, basil, and seasoning. Spoon a little onto the end of each slice of eggplant, and roll up. Place seam-side down in a greased oven-proof dish, bake for 15–17 minutes.

3   In a small pan, using a little of the dressing oil, sauté the tomato until softened. Add the remaining oil, balsamic vinegar and pine nuts, and gently warm. Season to taste. Arrange the rolls on a platter, and spoon the dressing over the rolls.

4   Garnish with fresh basil leaves to serve.

Serves 4

BROCCOLI AND CAULIFLOWER WITH HERB TOPPING

Ingredients

15g butter, cubed, plus extra for greasing
salt and black pepper
300g cauliflower, cut into florets
300g broccoli, cut into florets
1 1/2 tbsp olive oil

1 large clove garlic, finely chopped
3 tbsp coarse fresh white breadcrumbs
3 tbsp finely chopped fresh parsley
finely grated rind of 1 lemon and
1 small orange

Method

1 Preheat the oven to 230°C/Gas Mark 8. Lightly butter a shallow ovenproof dish. Bring a saucepan of lightly salted water to the boil. Add the cauliflower and cook for 2 minutes. Add the broccoli and cook for another 2–3 minutes, until the vegetables are tender but still firm to the bite. Drain.

2 Heat the oil in a small frying pan. Add the garlic, cook for 1 minute, then stir in the breadcrumbs and fry for a further minute, stirring, until they start to brown. Stir in the parsley and lemon and orange rind.

3 Arrange the cauliflower and broccoli in the dish and season well. Scatter over the breadcrumb and parsley mixture. Dot with butter, season again and bake near the top of the oven for 5 minutes or until the topping is golden.

Serves 6

SWEET POTATO AND ONION LAYERED BAKE

Ingredients

3 tbsp olive oil
3 onions, sliced into thin rings

750g sweet potato, thinly sliced
salt and black pepper
150mL chicken or vegetable stock

Method

1 Preheat the oven to 200°C/Gas Mark 6. Heat half the oil in a wok or large, heavy-based frying pan. Add the onions and fry for 8–10 minutes, until golden brown.

2 Arrange one-third of the sweet potatoes in an ovenproof dish and top with half the onions. Season and cover with another layer of sweet potato. Cover with the remaining onions, season, then finish with a final layer of sweet potatoes.

3 Pour over the stock over the sweet potatoes and onion, cover the dish with foil and bake for 40–45 minutes, until the potatoes are just tender. Remove the foil, and drizzle with the remaining oil. Increase the oven temperature to 230°C/Gas Mark 8 and bake for a further 8–10 minutes, until most of the liquid has evaporated and the top has browned.

Serves 6

SPINACH WITH SESAME SEEDS

Ingredients
**3 x 250g bags fresh spinach,
   stalks removed**
1 tbsp groundnut oil
1 tsp sesame oil
3 cloves garlic, chopped
2 tbsp sesame seeds
**juice of 1/2 lemon and 1/4 tsp finely
   grated lemon rind (optional)**
salt and black pepper

Method
1 Place the spinach in a large bowl, cover with boiling water, then leave for 2–3 minutes. Drain, then refresh under cold running water. Squeeze out any excess water, then coarsely chop.

2 Heat the groundnut and sesame oil in a wok or large, heavy-based frying pan. Add the garlic and the sesame seeds and fry for 1–2 minutes, until the garlic has begun to brown and the seeds have started to pop.

3 Stir in the spinach and fry for 1–2 minutes, until heated through. Add the lemon juice and rind (if using) season and mix well.

Serves 6

PUMPKIN WITH LEMON AND CHEESE SAUCE

Ingredients
**750g pumpkin or squash, peeled,
   deseeded and cut into chunks**
200mL chicken or vegetable stock
2 tsp arrowroot
**grated rind of 1/2 lemon and juice of
   1 lemon**
150g mature Cheddar, grated
2 tbsp chopped fresh dill or parsley
salt and black pepper

Method
1 Place the pumpkin or squash in a steamer or in a metal colander covered with foil. Set over a saucepan of simmering water and steam for 5–10 minutes, until tender but still firm.

2 Meanwhile, bring the stock to the boil in a small saucepan. Mix the arrowroot with the lemon juice until smooth, then stir in the lemon rind and add to the boiling stock. Simmer, stirring constantly, for 1–2 minutes, until the sauce thickens and looks glossy. Add 125g of the Cheddar and simmer for a further 1–2 minutes, until the cheese has melted. Stir in the dill or parsley, season, and mix well.

3 Preheat the grill to high. Transfer the pumpkin to a flameproof dish, pour over the lemon sauce and sprinkle with the reserved Cheddar. Place under the grill and cook for 5–8 minutes, until the sauce is bubbling and golden.

Serves 6

FRAGRANT PILAU RICE

Ingredients

large pinch of saffron strands
225g basmati rice
25g butter

1 shallot, finely chopped
3 cardamom pods
1 cinnamon stick
salt

Method

1 Briefly grind the saffron using a pestle and mortar, then mix the powder with 1 tablespoon of boiling water and set aside. Rinse the rice and drain.

2 Melt the butter in a large, heavy-based saucepan. Fry the shallot gently for 2 minutes or until softened. Add the cardamom pods, cinnamon and rice and mix well.

3 Add 300mL of water, the saffron mixture and salt. Bring to the boil, then reduce the heat and cover the pan tightly. Simmer the rice for 15 minutes or until the liquid has been absorbed and the rice is tender. Remove the cardamom pods and cinnamon stick before serving.

Serves 4

ROASTED VEGETABLES WITH MOZZARELLA

Ingredients

2 carrots, cut into matchsticks

2 small waxy potatoes, such
  as Charlotte, sliced

salt and black pepper

olive oil for brushing

1 red and 1 green pepper, each
  deseeded and cut into 8 pieces

1 aubergine, sliced

2 red onions, quartered

6 cloves garlic

150g ball mozzarella, grated

For the sauce

1 tbsp olive oil

1 small onion, finely chopped

2 cloves garlic, crushed

400g canned chopped tomatoes

1 tbsp tomato purée

1 tsp dried oregano

Method

1 Preheat the oven to 230°C/Gas Mark 8. Boil the carrots and potatoes in salted water for 2 minutes or until softened slightly, then drain.

2 To make the sauce, heat the oil in a heavy-based saucepan and cook the onion and garlic over a low heat for 5 minutes or until softened. Add the tomatoes, tomato purée and oregano. Bring to the boil, then reduce the heat and simmer, uncovered, for 20 minutes or until thickened.

3 Meanwhile, brush 2 large baking sheets with oil. Divide the carrots, potatoes, peppers, aubergine, onions and garlic between the sheets, arranging in a single layer on each. Brush with oil, season, then roast for 20 minutes or until softened.

4 Spread the tomato sauce over the base of an ovenproof dish and arrange the vegetables on top. Sprinkle with mozzarella and return to the oven for 5 minutes or until the cheese has melted.

Serves 4

CHEESY BAKED POTATO ROSTI

Ingredients

500g potatoes, peeled, grated and
  squeezed dry

bunch of spring onions, chopped

25g butter, melted

salt and black pepper

1 tsp groundnut oil

100g Gruyère, grated

Method

1 Preheat the oven to 200°C/Gas Mark 6. Place the potatoes and two-thirds of the onions in a bowl, add the butter and seasoning, then mix together well.

2 Heat the oil in an ovenproof frying pan. Place the potato mixture in the pan and press with the back of a spoon to make an even layer. Fry for 5–6 minutes, until the edges start to brown, then transfer to the oven and bake for 10 minutes or until the top has browned.

3 Increase the oven temperature to 230°C/Gas Mark 8. Mix the cheese with the remaining onions. Remove the pan from the oven and sprinkle the cheese and onion mixture over the rösti. Return to the oven and bake for 6–8 minutes, until the cheese is bubbling and golden.

Serves 6

GLAZED PEARS AND PARSNIPS

Ingredients

3 medium-sized parsnips
3 pears
1 tbsp butter
1 tbsp honey
1 tsp ground ginger
salt and freshly ground
black pepper

Method

1 Peel parsnips, then cut into 3 even lengths. Cut into julienne-like strips, avoiding the centre core in the upper section. Cut pears into 5cm-wide strips.

2 Heat butter in a frying pan, add parsnip strips and sauté gently until just soft. Use an egg slice to toss them over in the butter. Add pear strips and sauté a little longer. Add the honey, ginger, salt and pepper. Gently toss the pears and parsnips in the honey glaze to coat well. Remove to a warm serving dish.

Serves 4

PAK CHOI IN OYSTER SAUCE

Ingredients
400g pak choi
3 tbsp oyster sauce
I tbsp groundnut oil
salt

Method

I Trim the ends of the pak choi stalks, then separate the leaves and rinse thoroughly. Mix together the oyster sauce and oil.

2 Put the pak choi into a large saucepan of lightly salted boiling water and cook, uncovered, for 3 minutes or until tender. Drain thoroughly, return the pak choi to the pan, then add the oyster sauce and oil mixture and toss to coat evenly.

Serves 4

COURGETTE POLENTA SLICES

Ingredients
15g butter, plus extra for greasing
3 tbsp olive oil
250g courgettes, grated
750mL chicken or vegetable stock
175g instant polenta
salt and black pepper
40g Parmesan, finely grated

Method

I Grease a shallow 22cm square roasting tin. Heat the butter and I tablespoon of the oil in a large frying pan. Fry the courgettes for 3–4 minutes, stirring frequently, until softened but not browned. Remove from the heat.

2 Bring the stock to the boil in a large saucepan. Sprinkle in the polenta, stirring with a wooden spoon, and continue to stir for 5 minutes or until the polenta thickens and begins to come away from the sides of the pan. Remove from the heat and stir in the courgettes. Season to taste.

3 Tip the polenta into the roasting tin, spreading evenly, then sprinkle with Parmesan and leave for I hour to cool and set.

4 Heat a ridged cast-iron grill pan over a high heat. Cut the polenta into slices, brush with the rest of the oil and cook for 2–4 minutes on each side, until golden. Alternatively, cook under a preheated grill.

Serves 4

POTATO AND ONION DAUPHINOISE

Ingredients

10g butter, plus extra for greasing
675g baking potatoes
3 onions, thinly sliced

salt and black pepper
1 tsp freshly grated nutmeg
450mL single cream

Method

1 Preheat the oven to 180°C/Gas Mark 4. Butter a shallow ovenproof dish. Thinly slice the potatoes using the slicing blade on a food processor or with a sharp knife.

2 Arrange the potatoes and onions in alternate layers in the dish, lightly seasoning each layer with salt, pepper and nutmeg. Finish with a potato layer, then pour over the cream and dot with butter. Place on the lower shelf of the oven and cook for 1 hour or until golden brown.

Serves 4

BAKED PUMPKIN AND PEARS

Ingredients

400g butternut or Jap pumpkin
1 x 200g dried pears
¹/₃ cup water

¹/₂ tsp salt
freshly ground black pepper
2 tsp brown sugar
1 tbsp butter

Method

1 Cut pumpkin into 1cm slices, trim off skin. Place in a shallow, rectangular, ovenproof dish, overlapping alternately with the pears. Drizzle in the water, making sure all surface area is moistened. Sprinkle with salt, pepper and brown sugar. Dot the butter over the surface. Cover with foil, sealing around the edges. Place in a preheated moderate oven and cook 20 minutes.

2 Remove foil and return dish to the oven, uncovered, continue cooking for 5 to 10 minutes, until caramelised on top. Serve hot as an accompaniment to grilled meats or chicken.

Serves 4–6

SPICY CAULIFLOWER WITH GARLIC

Ingredients
2 slices brown bread
1 cauliflower, cut into florets
salt and black pepper
4 tbsp olive oil

1 clove garlic, crushed
1 red chilli, finely chopped
8 black olives, pitted and halved
1 tbsp capers

Method

1 Preheat the oven to 160°C/Gas Mark 3. Place the bread in the oven for 20 minutes or until it dries out and becomes crisp. Process in a food processor to make breadcrumbs. Alternatively, use a grater.

2 Place the cauliflower in a saucepan, cover with boiling water and add a little salt. Return to the boil, simmer for 1 minute or until slightly softened, then drain well.

3 Heat the oil in a large, heavy-based frying pan. Add the garlic, chilli and cauliflower and fry for 3 minutes or until the cauliflower starts to brown. Add the olives, capers, breadcrumbs and seasoning. Fry for a further 1 minute or until the breadcrumbs soak up the oil and flavour.

Serves 4

ORANGE-GLAZED CABBAGE

Ingredients
1 white cabbage, thinly sliced
For the glaze
juice of 2 oranges

2 tbsp maple syrup
1 tbsp olive oil
3 tbsp marmalade
1 tsp salt

Method

1 Preheat the oven to 200°C/Gas Mark 6. To make the glaze, place the orange juice, syrup, oil and marmalade in a large bowl and stir. Season, add the cabbage and mix to coat thoroughly.

2 Remove the cabbage from the bowl, reserving the glaze, and spread out on a large baking tray. Pour over half of the reserved glaze and cook for 15 minutes. Remove from the oven, toss the cabbage gently, then pour over the rest of the glaze. Return to the oven and bake for a further 10 minutes or until the cabbage has turned dark brown at the edges.

Serves 4

GARLIC AND POTATO MASH

Ingredients
1 kg large potatoes, cut into chunks
salt and black pepper
3 tbsp olive oil

2 heads of garlic, cloves separated and
  peeled
1 red onion, chopped
3 tbsp crème fraîche
4 tbsp snipped fresh chives

Method

1 Put the potatoes into a large saucepan of lightly salted boiling water, bring back to the boil, then simmer for 15–20 minutes, until tender.

2 Meanwhile, heat the oil in a heavy-based frying pan or saucepan over a low to medium heat. Add the garlic cloves, cover the pan and cook gently for 10–15 minutes, until tender and golden at the edges. Remove the garlic and set aside. Add the onion to the oil and cook for 10 minutes or until softened.

3 Drain the potatoes, then return to the pan and add the garlic, onion and oil. Mash well, then stir in the crème fraîche and chives and season to taste.

Serves 4

PAN-ROASTED PEPPERS WITH CAPERS AND VINEGAR

Ingredients
about 6 whole peppers of varying
  colours
6 tbsp olive oil

3 large cloves garlic, chopped finely
2 tbsp capers
2 tbsp wine or balsamic vinegar
salt

Method

1 Halve the peppers, flick out the seeds and cut into thick strips. Heat the oil in a wide frying pan and stir-fry the pepper strips over a high heat.

2 When the skins have begun to scorch at the edges add the garlic and capers. Fry for 30 seconds then add the vinegar and salt.

3 Let the vinegar sizzle for a minute then turn out on to a serving dish. Serve with crusty bread.

Serves 4

SWEET AND SOUR RED CABBAGE

Ingredients

3 tbsp olive oil

2 tbsp red wine vinegar

1 red or green chilli, sliced, seeds and
  pith included

grated rind and juice of 1 orange

1 tbsp orange-flower water

3 tbsp light muscovado sugar

1 red cabbage, thinly sliced

Method

1 Preheat the oven to 160°C/Gas Mark 3. Put the oil, vinegar, chilli, orange rind and juice, orange-flower water
and sugar into a small saucepan and simmer for 5 minutes.

2 Place the cabbage in an ovenproof casserole dish, then pour over the oil and vinegar mixture, reserving
about 2 tablespoons. Cover with a lid or double layer of foil and bake for 3 hours, checking the cabbage every
hour, and adding the remaining oil and vinegar mixture if it starts to dry out.

Serves 4

BABY NEW POTATOES WITH LEMON AND OLIVES

Ingredients

1 lemon
750g baby new potatoes, halved if large
2 cloves garlic, sliced
2 tbsp olive oil

salt and black pepper
15g butter
50g pitted green olives, quartered

Method

1 Preheat the oven to 220°C/Gas Mark 7. Halve the lemon. Squeeze the juice from 1 half and chop the other half into small pieces.

2 Toss the potatoes, lemon juice, chopped lemon, garlic and oil together. Season, then arrange in a single layer in a shallow roasting tin and dot with the butter. Cook for 25–30 minutes, shaking the tin occasionally, until the potatoes are tender and golden brown. Stir in the olives just before serving.

Serves 4

ASPARAGUS AND TOMATO WITH CUCUMBER SAUCE

Ingredients

1 large bunch asparagus (about 500g)
4 small ripe tomatoes
a selection of salad greens
For the cucumber sauce
1 small cucumber
1 tiny spring onion

salt
freshly ground pepper
1 1/2 tbsp lemon juice
1 tbsp sour cream
3 tbsp each salad oil and hazelnut
  or virgin olive oil
2 tbsp chopped dill

Method

1 First prepare the dressing. Peel the cucumber lightly and remove the seeds. Cut into chunks, roughly chop the onion and sprinkle them both with salt. Leave to drain for 1 hour in a colander. Rinse in cold water and drain again thoroughly. Puree in a blender or food processor, add salt, pepper, lemon juice, sour cream then lastly the oils, until a smooth dressing is formed. Add the dill and refrigerate.

2 Prepare and cook the asparagus and cut into 4cm pieces. Skin the tomatoes, halve them and remove the seeds. Cut each into strips. Arrange the salad greens on serving plates. Toss the asparagus and tomato in the dressing and arrange on each plate.

Serves 4

ROASTED BABY LEEKS WITH ORANGE AND GINGER

Ingredients

3 tbsp olive oil
3 tbsp balsamic vinegar
1 tsp grated orange rind
juice of 2 large oranges
12 baby leeks, halved lengthwise

150g shallots, chopped
1 tbsp grated root ginger
2 cloves garlic, chopped
salt
chopped fresh basil to garnish

Method

1 Preheat the oven to 200°C/Gas Mark 6. Mix together the oil, balsamic vinegar, orange rind and juice and pour into an ovenproof dish.

2 Add the leeks, shallots, ginger and garlic and toss gently to coat. Sprinkle with salt and cover loosely with foil. Cook for 25–30 minutes, until the leeks are just tender.

3 Increase the heat to 240°C/Gas Mark 9. Remove the foil and cook basting once for a further 10 minutes, or until the leeks have softened and most of the liquid has evaporated. Cool slightly, then sprinkle with basil and serve warm or cold.

Serves 6

CAMEMBERT FILO PARCELS

Ingredients

9 sheets filo pastry, cut into 30cm
  squares
150g butter, melted
3 tbsp chopped fresh rosemary,
  plus extra to garnish

3 x 250g round **Camembert cheeses**
black pepper
3 tbsp ready-made smooth apple sauce

Method

1 Lay a sheet of filo pastry on a work surface, then brush lightly with butter. Take a second sheet and place on top of the first sheet at an angle to form a star shape with 8 points. Brush with butter. Take a third sheet and place again at an angle, to add 4 more points to the star shape, then brush with butter.

2 Sprinkle a little rosemary over the star and place the Camembert in the centre. Top with black pepper, 1 tablespoon of the apple sauce and a little more rosemary.

3 Bring the edges of the filo up over the cheese, scrunch together to close at the top and brush with butter. Repeat for the other parcels. Cover loosely with cling film and refrigerate for 2 hours.

4 Preheat the oven to 200°C/Gas Mark 6. Lightly butter a large baking sheet. Put the parcels on the sheet and bake for 25 minutes or until crisp and golden. Cool for 15 minutes, then serve warm with rosemary sprinkled over.

Serves 20

LENTILS WITH WARM GARLIC OLIVE OIL

Ingredients

1 kg lentilles vertes
salt and black pepper
3 tbsp chopped fresh flat-leaf parsley
8 tbsp olive oil

3 cloves garlic, crushed
4 tbsp balsamic vinegar
5 spring onions, finely chopped
3 tbsp chopped fresh mint
2 tbsp snipped fresh chives

Method

1 Rinse the lentils in plenty of cold water, then drain well. Put into a large saucepan and cover generously with boiling water. Season lightly, bring to a simmer and add 2 tablespoons of the parsley. Cover and cook over a fairly low heat for 30 minutes or until tender, stirring occasionally and adding more boiling water if necessary.

2 In a frying pan, heat the oil over a low heat, add the garlic and fry for a few seconds to flavour the oil. Remove from the heat.

3 Drain the lentils and separate with a fork. Transfer to a serving bowl, spoon over the garlic oil and stir lightly. Sprinkle over the vinegar, then stir in the spring onions, remaining parsley, the mint and chives and season. Serve at room temperature.

Serves 20

Cooking is not an exact science: one does not require finely calibrated scales, pipettes and scientific equipment to cook, yet the conversion to metric measures in some countries has intimidated many a good cook.

Weights are given in the recipes in this book, but a few grams one way or another will not affect the success of your dish. Though recipes have been tested using the Australian Standard 250mL cup, 20mL tablespoon and 5mL teaspoon, they will work just as well with the US and Canadian 8fl oz cup, or the UK 300mL cup. We have used graduated cup measures in preference to tablespoon measures so that proportions are always the same. Where tablespoon measures have been given, these are not crucial measures, so using the smaller tablespoon of the US or UK will not affect the recipe's success. At least we all agree on the teaspoon size.

For breads, cakes and pastries, the only area which might cause concern is where eggs are used, as proportions will then vary. If working with a 250mL or 300mL cup, use large eggs (65g), adding a little more liquid to the recipe for 300mL cup measures if it seems necessary. Use the medium-sized eggs (55g) with 8fl oz cup measure. A graduated set of measuring cups and spoons is recommended, the cups in particular for measuring dry ingredients. Remember to level such ingredients to ensure their accuracy.

English measures

All measurements are similar to Australian with two exceptions: the English cup measures 300mL, whereas the Australian cup measure 250mL. The English tablespoon (the Australian dessertspoon) measures 14.8mL against the Australian tablespoon of 20mL.

American measures

The American pint is 16fl oz, a quart is equal to 32fl oz and the American gallon, 128fl oz. The Imperial measurement is 20fl oz to the pint, 40fl oz a quart and 160fl oz one gallon. The American tablespoon is equal to 14.8mL/^{1}/$_2$fl oz; the teaspoon is 5mL/^{1}/$_6$fl oz. The cup measure is 250mL/8^3/$_4$fl oz, the same as Australia.

Dry measures

All the measures are level, so when you have filled a cup or spoon, level it off with the edge of a knife. The scale below is the 'cook's equivalent'; it is not an exact conversion of metric to imperial measurement. To calculate the exact metric equivalent yourself, multiply ounces by 28.349523 to obtain grams, or divide by 28.349523 grams to obtain ounces.

Metric g = grams kg = kilograms	Imperial oz = ounces lb = pound
15g	^{1}/$_2$oz
20g	^{2}/$_3$oz
30g	1oz
55g	2oz
85g	3oz
115g	4oz/^{1}/$_4$ lb
125g	4^1/$_2$oz
140/145g	5oz
170g	6oz
200g	7oz
225g	8oz/^{1}/$_2$ lb
315g	11oz
340g	12oz/^{3}/$_4$ lb
370g	13oz
400g	14oz
425g	15oz
455g	16oz/1 lb
1,000g/1 kg	35.3oz/2.2 lb
1.5 kg	3.3 lb

Oven temperatures

The Celsius temperatures given here are not exact; they have been rounded off and are given as a guide only. Follow the manufacturer's temperature guide, relating it to oven description given in the recipe. Remember gas ovens are hottest at the top, electric ovens at the bottom and convection-fan forced ovens are usually even throughout. We included Regulo numbers for gas cookers which may assist. To convert °C to °F multiply °C by 9 and divide by 5 then add 32.

Oven temperatures

	C°	F°	Gas regulo
Very slow	120	250	1
Slow	150	300	2
Moderately slow	160	325	3
Moderate	180	350	4
Moderately hot	190–200	370–400	5–6
Hot	210–220	410–440	6–7
Very hot	230	450	8
Super hot	250–290	475–500	9–10

Cake dish sizes

Metric	Imperial
15cm	6in
18cm	7in
20cm	8in
23cm	9in

Loaf dish sizes

Metric	Imperial
23 x 12cm	9 x 5in
25 x 8cm	10 x 3in
28 x 18cm	11 x 7in

Liquid measures

Metric mL millilitres	Imperial fl oz fluid ounce	Cup and Spoon
5mL	$^1/_4$fl oz	1 tsp
20mL	$^2/_3$fl oz	1 tbsp
30mL	1fl oz	1 tbsp plus 2 tsps
55mL	2fl oz	$^1/_4$ cup
85mL	3fl oz	
115mL	4fl oz	$^1/_2$ cup
125mL	4$^1/_2$fl oz	
150mL	5$^1/_4$fl oz	
170mL	6fl oz	$^3/_4$ cup
225mL	8fl oz	1 cup
300mL	10$^1/_2$fl oz	
370mL	13fl oz	
400mL	14fl oz	1$^3/_4$ cups
455mL	16fl oz	2 cups
570mL	20fl oz	2$^1/_2$ cups
1L	35.3fl oz	4 cups

Cup measurements

One cup is equal to the following weights.

	Metric	Imperial
Almonds, flaked	85g	3oz
Almonds, kernel	155g	5$^1/_2$oz
Almonds, slivered, ground	125g	4$^1/_2$oz
Apples, dried, chopped	125g	4$^1/_2$oz
Apricots, dried, chopped	190g	6$^3/_4$oz
Breadcrumbs, packet	125g	4$^1/_2$oz
Breadcrumbs, soft	55g	2oz

	Metric	Imperial
Cheese, grated	115g	4oz
Choc bits	155$^1/_2$g	5oz
Coconut, desiccated	90g	3oz
Cornflakes	30g	1oz
Currants	155$^1/_2$g	5oz
Flour	115g	4oz
Fruit, dried (mixed, sultanas etc)	170g	6oz
Ginger, crystallised, glace	250g	8oz
Honey, treacle, golden syrup	315g	11oz
Mixed peel	225g	8oz
Nuts, chopped	115g	4oz
Prunes, chopped	225g	8oz
Rice, cooked	155g	5$^1/_2$oz
Rice, uncooked	225g	8oz
Rolled oats	90g	3oz
Sesame seeds	115g	4oz
Shortening (butter, margarine)	225g	8oz
Sugar, brown	155g	5$^1/_2$oz
Sugar, granulated or caster	225g	8oz
Sugar, sifted icing	155g	5$^1/_2$oz
Wheatgerm	60g	2oz

Length

Some of us still have trouble converting imperial length to metric. In this scale, measures have been rounded off to the easiest-to-use and most acceptable figures. To obtain the exact metric equivalent in converting inches to centimetres, multiply inches by 2.54 whereby 1 inch equals 25.4.

Metric mm=millimetres cm=centimetres	Imperial in = inches ft = feet
5mm, 0.5cm	$^1/_4$in
10mm, 1.0cm	$^1/_2$in
20mm, 2.0cm	$^3/_4$in
2.5cm	1in
5cm	2in
7$^1/_2$cm	3in
10cm	4in
12$^1/_2$cm	5in
15cm	6in
18cm	7in
20cm	8in
23cm	9in
25cm	10in
28cm	11in
30cm	12in, 1ft

GLOSSARY

al dente: Italian cooking term for ingredients that are cooked until tender but still firm to the bite; usually applied to pasta.
americaine: method of serving seafood – usually lobster and monkfish - in a sauce flavoured with olive oil, aromatic herbs, tomatoes, white wine, fish stock, brandy and tarragon.
anglaise: cooking style for simple cooked dishes such as boiled vegetables. Assiette anglaise is a plate of cold cooked meats.
antipasto: Italian for 'before the meal', it denotes an assortment of cold meats, vegetables and cheeses, often marinated, served as an hors d'oeuvre. A typical antipasto might include salami, prosciutto, marinated artichoke hearts, anchovy fillets, olives, tuna fish and Provolone cheese.
au gratin: food sprinkled with breadcrumbs, often covered with cheese sauce and browned until a crisp coating forms.
balsamic vinegar: a mild, extremely fragrant wine-based vinegar made in northern Italy. Traditionally, the vinegar is aged for at least seven years in a series of casks made of various woods.
baste: to moisten food while it is cooking by spooning or brushing on liquid or fat.
blanc: a cooking liquid made by adding flour and lemon juice to water in order to keep certain vegetables from discolouring as they cook.
blanch: to plunge into boiling water and then in some cases, into cold water. Fruits and nuts are blanched to remove skin easily.
blend: to mix thoroughly.
bouquet garni: a bunch of herbs, usually consisting of sprigs of parsley, thyme, marjoram, rosemary, a bay leaf, peppercorns and cloves, tied in muslin and used to flavour stews and casseroles.
braise: to cook whole or large pieces of poultry, game, fish, meat or vegetables in a small amount of wine, stock or other liquid in a closed pot. Often the main ingredient is first browned in fat and then cooked in a low oven or very slowly on top of the stove. Braising suits tough meats and older birds and produces a mellow, rich sauce.
broil: the American term for grilling food.
brown: cook in a small amount of fat until brown.
burghul (also bulgur): a type of cracked wheat, where the kernels are steamed and dried before being crushed.
buttered: to spread with softened or melted butter.
butterfly: to slit a piece of food in half horizontally, cutting it almost through so that when opened it resembles butterfly wings. Chops, large prawns and thick fish fillets are often butterflied so that they cook more quickly.
buttermilk: a tangy, low-fat cultured milk product whose slight acidity makes it an ideal marinade base for poultry.
calzone: a semicircular pocket of pizza dough, stuffed with meat or vegetables, sealed and baked.
caramelise: to melt sugar until it is a golden brown syrup.
champignons: small mushrooms, usually canned.
chasseur: (hunter) a French cooking style in which meat and chicken dishes are cooked with mushrooms, shallots, white wine, and often tomato.
clarify: to melt butter and drain the oil off the sediment.
coat: to cover with a thin layer of flour, sugar, nuts, crumbs, poppy or sesame seeds, cinnamon sugar or a few of the ground spices.
consomme: a clear soup usually made from beef.
coulis: a thin puree, usually of fresh or cooked fruit or vegetables, which is soft enough to pour (couler means to run). A coulis may be rough-textured or very smooth.
couscous: cereal processed from semolina into pellets, traditionally steamed and served with meat and vegetables in the classic North African stew of the same name.
croutons: small toasted or fried cubes of bread.
cream: to make soft, smooth and creamy by rubbing with back of spoon or by beating with mixer. Usually applied to fat and sugar.
cruciferous vegetables: certain members of the mustard, cabbage and turnip families with cross-shaped flowers and strong aromas and flavours.
crudités: raw vegetables, whether cut in slices or sticks to nibble plain or with a dipping sauce, or shredded and tossed as salad with a simple dressing.
cube: to cut into small pieces with 6 equal sides.
curdle: to cause milk or sauce to separate into solid and liquid. Example, overcooked egg mixtures.
daikon radish (also called mooli): a long white Japanese radish.
dark sesame oil (also called Oriental sesame oil): dark polyunsaturated oil with a low burning point, used for seasoning. Do not replace with lighter sesame oil.
deglaze: to dissolve congealed cooking juices or glaze on the bottom of a pan by adding a liquid, then scraping and stirring vigorously whilst bringing the liquid to the boil. Juices may be used to make gravy or to add to sauce.
degrease: to skim grease from the surface of liquid. If possible the liquid should be chilled so the fat solidifies. If not, skim off most of the fat with a large metal spoon, then trail strips of paper towel on the surface of the liquid to remove any remaining globules.
devilled: a dish or sauce that is highly seasoned with a hot ingredient such as mustard, Worcestershire sauce or cayenne pepper.
dice: to cut into small cubes.
dietary fibre: a plant-cell material that is undigested or only partially digested in the human body, but which promotes healthy digestion of other food matter.
dissolve: mix a dry ingredient with liquid until absorbed.
dredge: to coat with a dry ingredient such as flour or sugar.
drizzle: to pour in a fine thread-like stream over a surface.
dust: to sprinkle or coat lightly with flour or icing sugar.
Dutch oven: a heavy casserole with a lid usually made from cast iron or pottery.
emulsion: a mixture of two liquids that are not mutually soluble – for example, oil and water.
entree: in Europe, the 'entry' or hors d'oeuvre; in North America entree means the main course.
fillet: special cut of beef, lamb, pork or veal; breast of poultry and game; fish cut off the bone lengthwise.
flake: to break into small pieces with a fork.
flame: to ignite warmed alcohol over food.
fold in: a gentle, careful combining of a light or delicate mixture with a heavier mixture using a metal spoon.
garnish: to decorate food, usually with something edible.
glaze: a thin coating of beaten egg, syrup or aspic which is brushed over pastry, fruits or cooked meats.
gluten: a protein in flour that is developed when dough is kneaded, making it elastic.
gratin: a dish cooked in the oven or under the grill so that it develops a brown crust. Breadcrumbs or cheese may be sprinkled on top first. Shallow gratin dishes ensure a maximum area of crust.
grease: to rub or brush lightly with oil or fat.
infuse: to immerse herbs, spices or other flavourings in hot liquid to flavour it. Infusion takes from two to five minutes depending on the flavouring. The liquid should be very hot but not boiling.
joint: to cut poultry, game or small animals into serving pieces by dividing at the joint.
julienne: to cut food into match-like strips.
knead: to work dough using heel of hand with a pressing motion, while stretching and folding the dough.
line: to cover the inside of a container with paper, to protect or aid in removing mixture.
macerate: to soak food in liquid to soften.
marinade: a seasoned liquid, usually an oil and acid mixture, in which meats or other foods are soaked to soften and give more flavour.
marinara: Italian 'sailor's style' cooking that does not apply to any particular combination of ingredients. Marinara tomato sauce for pasta is most familiar.
marinate: to let food stand in a marinade to season and tenderise.
mask: to cover cooked food with sauce.
melt: to heat until liquified.
mince: to grind into very small pieces.
mix: to combine ingredients by stirring.
monounsaturated fats: one of three types of fats found in foods. They are believed not to raise the level of cholesterol in the blood.
nicoise: a garnish of tomatoes, garlic and black olives; a salad with anchovy, tuna and French beans is typical.
nonreactive pan: a cooking pan whose surface does not chemically react with food. Materials used include stainless steel, enamel, glass and some alloys.
noisette: small 'nut' of lamb cut from boned loin or rack that is rolled, tied and cut in neat slices. Noisette also means flavoured with hazelnuts, or butter cooked to a nut brown colour.
normande: a cooking style for fish, with a garnish of prawns, mussels and mushrooms in a white wine cream sauce; for poultry and meat, a sauce with cream, Calvados and apple.
olive oil: various grades of oil extract from olives. Extra virgin olive oil has a full, fruity flavour and the lowest acidity. Virgin olive oil is slightly higher in acidity and lighter in flavour. Pure olive oil is a processed blend of olive oils and has the highest acidity and lightest taste.
parboil: to boil or simmer until part cooked (i.e. cooked further than when blanching).
pare: to cut away the outside covering.
pâté: a paste of meat or seafood used as a spread for toast or crackers.
paupiette: a thin slice of meat, poultry or fish spread with a savoury stuffing and rolled. In the United States this is also called 'bird' and in Britain an 'olive'.
peel: to strip away outside covering.
plump: to soak in liquid or moisten thoroughly until full and round.
poach: to simmer gently in enough hot liquid to cover, using care to retain shape of food.
polyunsaturated fat: one of the three types of fats found in food. These exist in large quantities in such vegetable oils as safflower, sunflower, corn and soya bean. These fats lower the level of cholesterol in the blood.
puree: a smooth paste, usually of vegetables or fruits, made by putting foods through a sieve, food mill or liquefying in a blender or food processor.
ragout: traditionally a well-seasoned, rich stew containing meat, vegetables and wine. Nowadays, a term applied to any stewed mixture.
ramekins: small oval or round individual baking dishes.
reconstitute: to put moisture back into dehydrated foods by soaking in liquid.
reduce: to cook over a very high heat, uncovered, until the liquid is reduced by evaporation.
refresh: to cool hot food quickly, either under running water or by plunging it into iced water, to stop it cooking. Particularly for vegetables and occasionally for shellfish.
rice vinegar: mild, fragrant vinegar that is less sweet than cider vinegar and not as harsh as distilled malt vinegar. Japanese rice vinegar is milder than the Chinese variety.
roulade: a piece of meat, usually pork or veal, that is spread with stuffing, rolled and often braised or poached. A roulade may also be a sweet or savoury mixture that is baked in a Swiss roll tin or paper case, filled with a contrasting filling, and rolled.
rubbing-in: a method of incorporating fat into flour, by use of fingertips only. Also incorporates air into mixture.
safflower oil: the vegetable oil that contains the highest proportion of polyunsaturated fats.
salsa: a juice derived from the main ingredient being cooked or a sauce added to a dish to enhance its flavour. In Italy the term is often used for pasta sauces; in Mexico the name usually applies to uncooked sauces served as an accompaniment, especially to corn chips.
saturated fats: one of the three types of fats found in foods. These exist in large quantities in animal products, coconut and palm oils; they raise the level of cholesterol in the blood. As high cholesterol levels may cause heart disease, saturated fat consumption is recommended to be less than 15% of kilojoules provided by the daily diet.
sauté: to cook or brown in small amount of hot fat.
score: to mark food with cuts, notches of lines to prevent curling or to make food more attractive.
scald: to bring just to boiling point, usually for milk. Also to rinse with boiling water.
sear: to brown surface quickly over high heat in a hot dish.
seasoned flour: flour with salt and pepper added.
sift: to shake a dry, powdered substance through a sieve or sifter to remove any lumps and give lightness.
simmer: to cook food gently in liquid that bubbles steadily just below boiling point so that the food cooks in even heat without breaking up.
singe: to quickly flame poultry to remove all traces of feathers after plucking.
skim: to remove a surface layer (often of impurities and scum) from a liquid with a metal spoon or small ladle.
slivered: sliced in long, thin pieces, usually refers to nuts, especially almonds.
soften: re gelatine – sprinkle over cold water and allow to gel (soften) then dissolve and liquefy.
souse: to cover food, particularly fish, in wine vinegar and spices and cook slowly; the food is cooled in the same liquid. Sousing gives food a pickled flavour.
steep: to soak in warm or cold liquid in order to soften food and draw out strong flavours or impurities.
stir-fry: to cook thin slices of meat and vegetable over a high heat in a small amount of oil, stirring constantly to even cooking in a short time. Traditionally cooked in a wok, however a heavy based frying pan may be used.
stock: a liquid containing flavours, extracts and nutrients of bones, meat, fish or vegetables.
stud: to adorn with; for example, baked ham studded with whole cloves.
sugo: an Italian sauce made from the liquid or juice extracted from fruit or meat during cooking.
sweat: to cook sliced or chopped food, usually vegetables, in a little fat and no liquid over very low heat. Foil is pressed on top so that the food steams in its own juices, usually before being added to other dishes.
thicken: to make a thin, smooth paste by mixing together arrowroot, cornflour or flour with an equal amount of cold water; stir into hot liquid, cook, stirring until thickened.
toss: to gently mix ingredients with two forks or fork spoon.
total fat: the individual daily intake of all three fats previously described in this glossary. Nutritionists recommend that fats provide no more than 35% of the energy in the diet.
udonji: udon stock.
vine leaves: tender, lightly flavoured leaves of the grapevine, used in ethnic cuisine as wrappers for savoury mixtures. As the leaves are usually packed in brine, they should be well rinsed before use.
whip: to beat rapidly, incorporate air and produce expansion.
zest: thin outer layer of citrus fruits containing the aromatic citrus oil. It is usually thinly pared with a vegetable peeler, or grated with a zester or grater to separate it from the bitter white pith underneath.

INDEX